A Kinesthetic Homiletic

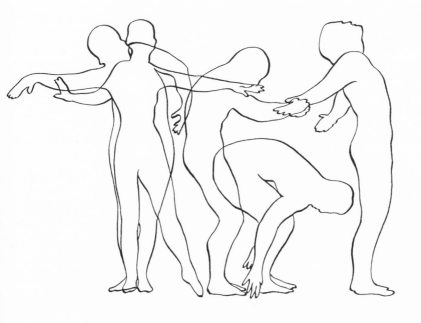

A Kinesthetic

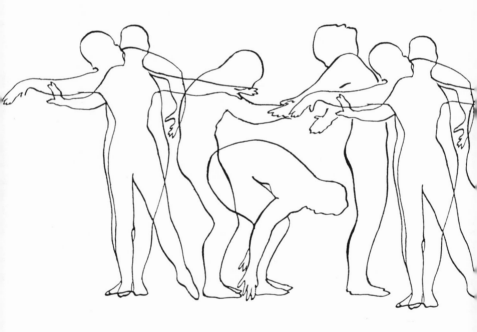

Pamela Ann Moeller

Homiletic

Embodying Gospel in Preaching

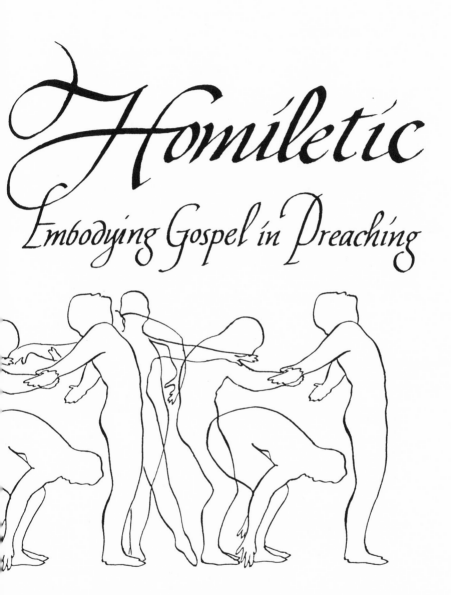

Fortress Press ❖ Minneapolis

To my parents,
who started this dance

Library of Congress Cataloging-in-Publication Data

Moeller, Pamela Ann, 1947–
    A kinesthetic homiletic : embodying Gospel in preaching / Pamela Ann Moeller.
        p.   cm.
    Includes bibliographical references and index.
    ISBN 0-8006-2650-8 (alk. paper)
    1. Preaching.   2. Movement, Psychology of—Religious aspects—Christianity.   3. Dancing—Religious aspects—Christianity.
I. Title.
BV4221.M64   1993
246'.7—dc20   92-31711
                                                                                    CIP

The paper used in this publication meets the minimum requirements of American National Standard for Information Sciences—Permanence of Paper for Printed Library Materials, ANSI Z329.48-1984.   ∞™

Manufactured in the U.S.A.   AF 1-2650

97   96   95   94   93   1   2   3   4   5   6   7   8   9   10

CONTENTS

ILLUSTRATIONS

viii

ACKNOWLEDGMENTS

Simon Hanson and the late Harris Kaasa, for opening up theology to me.

George Landes, for teaching me exegesis and empowering me to find gospel in the Hebrew Scriptures.

Walter Burghardt, S.J., embodier of gospel *par excellence.*

Chester Hertling, for teaching me how to dance and for her helpful comments on this manuscript.

Don Wardlaw, for enabling me to discover how to dance in the pulpit and for his instructive advice.

John Riggs, and many members of the Academy of Homiletics, with whom I have done glorious dancing and whose conversation, writing, and preaching have served as counterpoint and catalyst.

Fred Craddock and Don Saliers, who both required scholarship from me and freed me to push the bounds of tradition.

My students, for daring to believe in me and risking their egos to discover a kinesthetic homiletic really does work.

Fred and Darlene Harrison, for the photography that made the illustrations possible.

All those who have one way or another been somewhere along the way a partner in gospel choreography, not the least of these my editors, Timothy Staveteig and Lois Torvik.

Thanks be to God

The Motion of God and Human Movement

Then the word of God came to Elijah, saying, "Go now to Zarephath . . . and live there; for I have commanded a widow there to feed you." So Elijah went. When he came to the gate of the town, a widow was there gathering sticks. Elijah called to her, "Bring me a little water in a vessel so that I may drink. Bring me a morsel of bread in your hand." But she said, "I have nothing baked, only a handful of meal in a jar, and a little oil in a jug; I am gathering sticks so that I may go home and prepare it for myself and my child, that we may eat it and die." Elijah said to her, "First make me a little cake and bring it to me, and afterward make something for yourself and your child. For thus says the God of Israel, The jar of meal will not be emptied and the jug of oil will not fail until the day that God sends rain on the earth." She did as Elijah said. The jar of meal never emptied, neither did the jug of oil fail. 1 Kings 17:8-16 (NRSV, adapted).

We feel the rhythms—the rhythm of the diaphragmatic wailing of a hungry child, the rhythm of rocking in despair, the rhythm of sluggish, weary walking, of hypoglycemic shaking, of picking up sticks, of bend and reach and step and bend and reach and step.

We sense the motion—the motion of putting one foot in front of the other, of shimmering mirage, of labored, dehydrated breathing, of slogging out of the wilderness, of a bucket being hand-over-handed up the well, of ill-advised gulping of water down a parched and sore throat.

1

Our muscles contract and release through the day-after-day going to the cupboard, in reaching up and bringing down the jug and then the jar, in kneading and pouring, in giving and taking, in chewing and swallowing.

We move the rhythm of questions asked and answered, of pour and dip and wash; we sense the motion of gathering Sunday by Sunday; we feel the flow of hymn and prayer, the contract/release of work and play, the up, down, in and out of life in the global community.

The movement goes on without end, and in endless variations. The movement is the motion of God being there for us, the rhythm of God embodied for us in mothers who give us shelter, who rock us to sleep, who keep us clean and dry and fed. The movement is the kinesthesia of God embodied in prophets who call us to account and envision our future; of God embodied in helpless infants whose only talent seems to be coaxing an impossible smile out of us as we reach beyond ourselves to be whatever they need us to be.

Left to our self-sufficiency we would all be dead. But God is there for us, God moving in pastors and pew-sitters, parents and children, neighbors and strangers from distant lands; God embodied in everyone who lives only a face, a hand, a heart of God away from death; God embodied in everyone whose face, hands, heart stand between us and death.[1]

This is a book about embodying gospel in our congregation and in our global community, about embodying gospel for anyone and everyone who is a heart, face, hand of God away from death. It came into being because I have trouble making the transition from hearing a sermon on Sunday morning to living gospel all the rest of the week. Words, concepts, appeals to my intellect, no matter how wonderful, are rarely enough for me. At the very least, in my moments of deepest distress I have needed more than wonderful words of love. I have needed God embodied in hands that bathed me, hands that put bread in my hands; I have needed God embodied in arms that held me together and held me up; I have needed God embodied in a nod of a head that could assure me from across the room that I am still God's beloved. I have needed . . . God embodied for me. I am not alone in this.

This book about embodying gospel arises out of more than my need; it grows as well out of gracious experience. God has been there for me, in the heart, hands, face, feet, of family, friends, teachers, students,

---

1. This material is drawn from a sermon preached on the occasion of the baptism of Katharine Louise Henry Rodgers, Melville, Saskatchewan.

and oftentimes strangers. God has been there for me: I have been bathed, fed, healed, held up in my weakness, set free to dance—by human movements that have lived gospel, that have embodied God for me. Moreover, even though I have difficulty moving from hearing a sermon on Sunday morning to living gospel the rest of the week, on one or two occasions I have been blessed with the opportunity and the ability to be the arms or legs of God for someone else. I am no longer willing for such moments to be either rare or serendipitous, and so, with this book, I hope to help my readers to create such events often.

Along with focusing on gospel, this book centers on kinesthesia. This term does not mean just movement—kinetics—but movement *and* the sensory experience and memory that result from movement[2] and, which I submit, generate new movement. Gospel calls those who are engaged in homiletical enterprise to fully act out of what we are: the temple of the spirit, incarnational—not just speakers of gospel message, but doers of gospel, embodiers of God through the sermon as well as in the world. I think we are long overdue in bringing theology and physicality, thought, movement and its sensory memory, sermons, and gospel embodiments together intentionally and honoring them as a coherent whole.

What does it mean to conceive of a sermon not just as conveying messages intellect to intellect, but as doing gospel body to body? More importantly, what does that kind of embodied gospel look like, and how do we do it with authentic, faithful intentionality? I propose one vision here in answer to these questions. But I hope, finally, that this book is more than a book about gospel and kinesthesia, and more than a vision of embodied gospel. I hope finally that it does what it says and shows, that it embodies gospel, embodies God—not in itself, but in its readers. I think the survival of the world and our global family depends on such embodiment.

I write for anyone in our global community who is one face, hand, body of God away from death, and for anyone who would embody gospel for those who are in that predicament. I address preachers, and teachers of preachers, and students of preaching. I also hope people in the pew will read this book, because such folk are, perhaps more than the rest, preachers and students and teachers of preachers, and because every one of us, no matter what our daily work, is called to embody gospel.

Perhaps you think that this book is not for you because you are nervous about your body, because you think you have two left feet, because your knees (real or metaphorical) are weak or plagued with

---

2. *Webster's Ninth New Collegiate Dictionary.*

arthritis, or because you travel in a wheelchair. Or perhaps you have danced for years on stage or in ballrooms or in the privacy of your own home, and the notion of combining dance and preaching seems either utterly absurd to you—or the most natural thing in the world. Whatever the case, this book invites all of us to love our bodies for what they are, the gift of God by which we embody God in the world, however much or little we think our bodies are capable of. It invites us to discover the possibilities of intentionally combining kinesthesia and homiletics. It offers, I hope, empowerment for becoming more fully what we are meant to be—Christ for one another, embodiers of gospel, embodying God in our global community.

Illustrations are included, most of them in the section that deals with particular dance steps and technique (chapter 3). The drawings are not meant to model the "right way" of doing things movement-wise, but to advance suggestions about direction and form, as well as to give some wisdom about how to avoid injury. Readers can do kinesthetic homiletics without the specific modern dance steps and the technique utilized here. All of us already own most of the movements, even though many of us do not know that. Putting the movement to work in the homiletic endeavor is thus largely a matter of attending to our bodies and applying our imaginations. The steps and technique, discussion and illustration are meant as catalysts and visions of possibilities that only readers can finally define.

Sermon manuscripts are not included. Kinesthetic homiletic sermons reduce to print less authentically than any other kind, and with as much difficulty, if not more, as does choreography. When we take embodiment of gospel seriously, and consider all the dynamics of text and preacher and congregation in *their particular embodiments and relationships* in this time and place, trying to put such a sermon in print is like trying to put time in a bottle. There is no way to prove the pudding other than by taking one's courage and trust in hand and doing homiletics kinesthetically. That means that the end of this work lives in the readers' imaginations, intellects, hands, feet, rib cages . . . *chutzpah*? Yes.

I trust such an end will come to pass, perhaps because this volume does what it says, but foremost and finally because gospel stands outside our doors, inviting us to dance. Gospel offers to set us free from our fears and our needs, offers to empower us to become the hands, face, feet of God for our world.

Let the movement begin.

1

Discovering the Integration of Gospel and Self

Life begins with movement. God creates, the Spirit hovers. Gametes move from one body part to another, from body to body, and in integrated form out into the world. A baby wriggles, rolls, crawls, scoots, walks, runs, skips its way into adulthood. Neurons dance. An arm reaches for and opens a book; a hand slides pen across paper; a body makes its way into a gathered community. Diaphragm contracts, releases; mouth opens, words are propelled by waves that bounce against eardrums. Eyebrows elevate, shoulders slouch . . .

In the second year of my pastoral ministry I took up modern dance under the tutelage of a member of my congregation. It was a revelatory experience. After years of training my mind toward coherent, articulate theological thinking and expression, I discovered that my body also was a voice, a voice without words, but one capable of expression quite beyond the abilities of my mind and mouth. Astonished by this gift, I went on to explore jazz and ballet. Along the way it became clear to me that dance had something fundamental to say and do in our worship life that was not being said/done in all the diversity of hymns, sermons, prayers, baptism, and supper. As a result of that conviction, I became a choreographer and performer of sacred dance in a variety of worship contexts. I danced prayers, preludes, and offertories, even Scripture, and enabled congregations to find their own movement in hymnody. I began to have a hunch that there is an essential link between dance and preaching that makes dance essential to preaching—although I am not at all certain if the reverse is true. I now believe that if we are indeed going to preach, or if we are going to enable others to participate in the preaching enterprise, we must first learn to dance, and teach those who would participate in gospel to dance.

A theology that claims communication begins with sound originating in God's saying via *dabar* and *logos*[1] has enamored us of the word. Bolstered by the printing press and rationalism, this theology shapes a homiletical praxis that reveals itself to be caught up in a love affair between the intellect and the oral/aural.[2] Yet something essential is missing: God creating and the Spirit hovering—and the necessity for human muscles, at least, as well as sound waves, to move before a word can be pronounced or heard, and probably before it can even be thought.[3]

Perhaps this neglect of movement is why people accuse preachers of not practicing what we preach. If our preaching is not consciously and intentionally grounded in our bodily experience, can our words be more than empty? Immediately we hear a voice crying out about the objective truth of some words, or the absolute truth of gospel, which stands on its own as valid apart from our behavior. Yet words are never objective, and neither is gospel. Both have to do with communication between beings, whole persons engaged in relationships with other embodied individuals. Words and gospel have to do with subjectivity: God and humankind, you and I, interrelating as subjects. Nevertheless, how quickly we overlook the "angel" who wrestled with Jacob and the word embodied in the prophets. How quickly we forget incarnation!

The fact is that word and act/movement cannot be addressed separately, as anyone who signs or reads Braille, or even watches others do either of these activities, must surely recognize. Nor can either speech or movement have primacy over the other, because we are embodied beings, moving somewhere, somehow, no matter how immobile we think we are. Still, we act before we speak and as we speak, thereby forming our speech out of movement.[4] Therefore, we need a homiletic that understands, works from, and manifests a clear sense that preaching grows

1. John 1:1; see Arthur Van Seters, "Preaching as an Oral/Aural Act." Papers of the Annual Meeting of the Academy of Homiletics, 1989, for example.
2. Most of the vast collection of homiletical literature reflects this emphasis on the word. Among more recent publications, for example, are: David Buttrick, *Homiletic: Moves and Structures* (Philadelphia: Fortress Press, 1987); John S. McClure, *The Four Codes of Preaching: Rhetorical Strategies* (Minneapolis: Fortress Press, 1991); Thomas G. Long, *The Witness of Preaching* (Louisville: Westminster/John Knox Press, 1989); Walter Brueggemann, *Finally Comes the Poet: Daring Speech for Proclamation* (Minneapolis: Fortress Press, 1989). Brueggemann says, "The meeting of the community of faith is a speech meeting" (7).
3. One needs only to visit the sound wave machine at the nearest science museum to recognize that sound is a physical *movement*.
4. Chris Smith's weaving metaphor rightly pulls us into the tactile and movement realm, for the weaver has to move to thread the loom and push the shuttle through. Yet this

out of the wholeness of being: God's, yes, but also our very subjective, nonrational, sometimes erratic, disordered, and undeniably embodied selves engaged in dynamic relationship with God and most particularly with and through God's family.

The homiletical enterprise *is* on the move, and in the right directions. We recognize that preaching is a whole-body activity, dependent as much on a healthy diaphragm, an expressive face, and appropriate gestures (many preachers today eschew the pulpit because it obstructs the full-bodied proclamation of gospel) as well as on a clear theme and purpose and a well-constructed form for our sermons. Out of an expository, concept-oriented preaching style we see evidence that preaching increasingly aims at sensory expression of gospel that does not just talk about the text but strives to show it, endeavors to create experiences with "hearers"[5] around a text. Don Wardlaw's question of "what grace looks like when it walks around"[6] manifests this experiential awareness, as does Tom Troeger's reminder that "people process a sermon with all of themselves," from swinging foot to back slouching into the pew to rising eyebrows.[7] We remember that congregations are made up of persons with eyes and noses as well as ears. We try to paint pictures with our words so that our people will see the parade of feast-fare into Wisdom's house and get a whiff or two of fragrant bread just baked and of aromatic, spicy wine (Prov. 9:1ff.).

Troeger goes so far as to propose a definition of homiletics as "theology processed through the body."[8] He urges us to image scenes that do what our text does[9] and to think in terms of television when we consider sermon formation.[10] Yet even so, our imagining too easily remains in our heads. No matter how colorful and lively our creativity there may be, we are all too likely to continue to engage in endeavor that is only or primarily mental. Moreover, even the medium of television is a flat

---

metaphor still presupposes an "other" that is not in itself being; our kinesthetic is not a conscious and intentional part of sermon development. We are left with the subject/object split of word/act and continue to function only in our heads when it comes to actual sermon preparation. Christine Smith, *Weaving the Sermon: Preaching in a Feminist Perspective* (Louisville: Westminster/John Knox Press, 1989).

5. "Hearers" is clearly an inadequate term for members of congregations who engage with us in the preaching enterprise, particularly when we are talking about experience and embodiment. A more appropriate term might be co-participants, bulky though that is.

6. In his "Growth in Preaching" seminar taken as part of my D.Min. work at McCormick Theological Seminary in the early eighties.

7. Thomas H. Troeger, "Emerging New Standards in the Evaluation of Effective Preaching," *Worship* 64, no. 4 (1990): 294.

8. Troeger, "Emerging New Standards," 294.

9. Thomas H. Troeger, "Shaping Sermons by the Encounter of Text with Preacher," in Don M. Wardlaw, ed., *Preaching Biblically* (Philadelphia: Westminster Press, 1983), 153ff.

10. Thomas H. Troeger, *Imagining a Sermon* (Nashville: Abingdon Press, 1990).

and passive one that allows us to continue to ignore our own bodily kinesthesia even while considering someone else's. Worse, we can remote-control it off, and ignore movement altogether.

So for the most part, the processes most preachers use to prepare sermons are first and foremost cerebral, intellectual exercises and not embodied ones. We have not yet caught the spirit of the dance. Our preaching is still mostly head to head, even for those of us who attend to intuitive patterns of working, exercise the imagination, focus on the narrative or televisual approach. We are not yet putting our whole beings to work in the homiletic enterprise. Our preaching continues to be constructed out of the grammar and syntax of words, sentences, paragraphs (even among those of us who preach in poetic mode). We still function out of the mind-body/subject-object split. Hence we can speak of word *and* sacrament, homiletics *and* liturgy—worse, worship *and* preaching—and do homiletics largely in the brain. To the degree that we do so, I submit, we continue to live as disintegrated beings.

We can no longer get away with this disintegrative, disembodied proclamation of gospel. Gospel has never endorsed this kind of proclamation, if we are honest about it, and neither will the people in our congregations. Jesus did not merely talk about the commonwealth of God; he handed out bread, fish, and wine for its feast, laid hands on the sick and dying, walked as he talked, reached down and picked up children, and probably hugged those who simply needed to be loved. As contemporary people grow more and more aware of the environment and the interconnectedness of ecosystems, we increasingly value our own personal physicality. Health centers and sports clubs have proliferated, and the variety of athletic shoes and related apparel on the market seems to be growing as fast as the national debt. Some of this emphasis on the body is media hype, but many people raised in the church are clearly voting with their feet, preferring the activity of the golf course or the tennis court or even vigorous charismatic worship to the passivity of the main-line pew. No doubt many messages can be drawn from this trend, but we can no longer afford to ignore the need to attend to human physicality. Disembodied gospel simply will not do.

Troeger calls us to intentional use of our senses in the homiletic endeavor and encourages us to "feel the bodily weight of truth"[11] by experiencing the somatic aspects of the text. He is right on target. But we need to do more than this. We need to become fully kinesthetic

11. Ibid., p. 53ff.

homileticians. We are called and empowered to do this by gospel that is itself incarnational.

I think it will help to put flesh on this idea of kinesthetic homiletics if I begin by characterizing several types of dance, taking some poetic license in regard to hyperbole and stereotyping. These descriptions are based on personal bodily experience with each of the forms described, not on technical definitions or formal academic research. They are unapologetically subjective, and others may well hold quite different perspectives developed from their own equally valid and important experiences.

Classical ballet consists, to a large degree, of set and inflexible steps that are combined in various ways to make dances for specific musical pieces. Moreover, there are unbreakable rules: the dancer must not bend the torso; the toes are kept pointed except when the feet are flat on the floor; the hands are "ballet hands" unless they have some particular function such as holding or lifting. Even the apparel is relatively fixed; a ballerina, for example, wears leotard, tights, and tutu or filmy skirt. Body shapes are prescribed as long and lean, and women's hair is done up in a bun atop the head. Classical ballet inevitably features a relatively renowned prima ballerina, shown off to advantage by a male dancer, augmented by a *corps de ballet*. To participate in this art, a dancer must train for years and years to achieve the physical perfection required. The prime of the dancer's career is usually very short and ends at a very young age. Seasoned dancers suffer feet brutalized by wooden point shoes; knees, hips, and spinal column ravaged by the extremes of extension, by leaps and landings. One always knows pretty much what to expect from a classical ballet—the only question is how technically perfect and how "artistically" the steps will be performed.

Modern dance, on the other hand, is comprised of the possibilities of movement. Indeed, there are particular principles: Martha Graham's famous "contract-release" (which is simply what human muscles *do*), and the acceptability of all levels and directions of space for any kind of movement. So, the modern dancer might *pirouette* (roll), inch or wiggle along the floor, on knees or feet, or in the air. Movements may be generated by a particular piece or moment of music, or by listening to the inner being. The costume suits the whole dance. It can be anything from bare skin to a "tent" or tube that encloses a whole company of dancers. Modern dance prescribes no body shapes or sizes and no prime age, although the vigor and flexibility common to modern dance will tend to focus in the young—yet one can start dancing at 40 and dance wonderfully for many years. There are no wrong moves in modern dance, although there are moves that do not say or do what is intended and moves that are not suited to a particular body. While modern dance may include featured dancers, the overall effect is often one of essential equality among the entire company. One never knows what to expect from modern dance, except an experience that is almost guaranteed to touch and move one rather dramatically—not always happily, sometimes downright scandalously (hardly inappropriate for gospel!), often astonishingly and wonderfully.

In between these two styles of dance stands modern ballet, which takes classical ballet as its starting point and admits to its salon some limited aspects of modern dance. Modern ballet takes liberties with classical ballet, but it does not know the freedom and naturalness of modern dance, and it is not likely to be on the cutting edge of life. To my mind, modern ballet moves conservatively, endeavoring to keep classical ballet alive, perhaps past its prime. If classical ballet is cold, and modern dance hot, modern ballet is a definite Laodicean lukewarm (Rev. 3:14-22).

Preaching that is highly cerebral, highly structured, proceeding step-by-step following all the rules, is best compared to classical ballet. That is not to say this kind of preaching is without positive value. Classical ballet does, after all, continue to entrance audiences—perhaps precisely because of its demand for a high degree of technical skill, and for its precision, clarity, and reliability. Nevertheless, when the same preacher wearing the same robe or alb gets into the same pulpit Sunday after Sunday and presents a rationally constructed sermon full of precision and predictability . . . How often do most of us want to attend classical ballet? More importantly, how many of us can dance one?

Identifying the preaching comparable to modern dance is more difficult. I think that Jeremiah preached this way, and there was one Sunday in Emory University's Cannon Chapel when the season was penitential Lent, but the worship (including the sermon!) was so Easter for me that while I have long forgotten the preacher and the words, I will never forget the experience of resurrection that left me laughing and ecstatic. Such preaching is always passionate, but not all passionate preaching fits in this category. Modern-dance preaching may be quiet or vivacious, fast-paced or ambling, but it is never dull. Such preaching is quite likely to be scandalous and rarely, if ever, defined primarily by rules. It is theology that is more than processed through the body, it is *generated* in the body by those who permit spirit, gospel, and self to integrate—at least as fully as any of us can ever hope for.

Preaching that is like modern ballet grows out of preaching that is like classical ballet. In other words, its fundamental processes are the cerebral, rational, academic, and rule-defined ones. But because we know we are speaking to whole persons, we reach into the studio of modern dance to find ways to cast our themes in more imaginative molds than static language provides, and sometimes to find different ways to put the sequences of steps together. Or, in a moment of desperation we might dabble with the essence of modern-dance preaching in the hope of ending our writer's block. In any case, what we get is a classically trained ballerina with her point shoes replaced by bare feet and her tutu eschewed for a jersey tunic. Meanwhile the inner content, thought patterns, and processes are essentially the same because all we have done is impose something externally expanded on what is intrinsically classical-ballet preaching.

The degree to which most of us have moved from classical homiletic theory toward kinesthetic homiletic is at best compared to modern ballet, clearly a step in the right direction. But if this is as far as we go, I daresay we come under the judgment promised the church at Laodicea. Thanks be to God, the same text also tells us that gospel stands outside our door, knocking and waiting for us to let it in, eager to free us of our inhibitions and guilt so that we might break bread together and participate in festal choreography.

I do not propose a kinesthetic homiletic that is nothing other than an abandonment of all we hold dear for the unknown frontiers of energy applied to inner or outer space and time. What I do suggest, rather, is that if we are truly faithful to the inevitable and indivisible whole of act/word (most commonly expressed as word/act) and body/mind, we will always begin each step of the sermon development process with movement as well as with reason,[12] and we will sustain our homiletic enterprise throughout with movement. We will ask what this text is *doing*, perhaps even before we ask what it is *saying*. Our means of discovering the answers will be grounded in body movements through

---

12. See Don M. Wardlaw, ed., *Learning Preaching: Understanding and Participating in the Process* (Lincoln, Ill.: Lincoln Christian College and Seminary Press, 1989), chap. 9. This chapter is entitled "Video as a Resource for the Process." It discusses the use of video in the homiletical classroom and includes a variety of suggestions for actively dialoguing with Scripture. While the intention here is to "help students embody the reality they present in their sermons," p. 160, activity is focused on the visual. I am more interested in the student *feeling* the movement and being grounded in a kinesthesia and a kinesthetic hermeneutic. For that reason I do not use video in the sermon development process. Moreover, Wardlaw suggests students can make sensory connections "in immobile, meditative solitude" or by "sculpting" some aspect of the text or its impact on the student. On the contrary, a kinesthetic homiletic recognizes that none of us is ever immobile and that even the most limited movement available to us expands our awareness beyond conception. Nevertheless, the author of this chapter is moving in much the same direction as my work, and the chapter is a helpful resource for teachers of preaching.

which we seek to kinesthetically feel in motor activity what is happening in this pericope. Rather than initiating our exegesis by analyzing the text, we will allow the pericope to choreograph our bodies. We will discover the form of the passage by discovering how it moves the body through it. We will ask our questions of context by moving among our people and by attending to how they move through life. Always our processes will shape themselves out of physical activity that is essentially natural to us (body movement) rather than out of movement imposed on us by the current homiletical logicians, gurus, or possibly, choreographers.

The point is not to turn the brain off but to turn the body on, to enable it to be a full partner in the *pas de Dieu*. The point is not to throw away all the wonderful schemes and processes we have learned for exegesis and sermon formation but to use them to check and support our body-work. The point is not to replace the preached sermon with a wordless dance but to create the preached sermon out of the dance choreographed by the text.

An embodied gospel, a kinesthetic homiletic, does not occur by putting movement on after all the mind-work is done, adding just the right gesture (in the way illustrations used to be used), or even by our dabbling with movement here and there along the way. A kinesthetic homiletic grows as we begin and continue with the movement the text inspires in us, no matter how self-conscious or awkward we feel. A kinesthetic homiletic lives out what Calvin always understood: that Scripture is not the word of God for us by the coming together of text and person; it becomes the word of God for us when the Spirit moves the word in us and moves *us*.[13]

The fact is, we already begin sermon preparation kinesthetically, with electrons dancing in our brains, summoning our muscles to contract and release as we reach up to take the Bible down from the shelf and open it. Our eyes and nerves send signals pulsing down the pathways of our neurological network, and this being that never ceases to bustle with activity responds to the words with hurried-up breathing, blood rushing in excitement, or stomachs cramping and sinking in dread, nerves humming and muscles flexed, even as we sit still in our chairs. Eventually, we do continue with movement as we punch typewriter or computer keys and shuffle pages and get up to proclaim. But this is not yet embodied gospel, because we remain largely unconscious of the fact

13. Pamela Ann Moeller, "Worship in John Calvin's 1559 Institutes: With a View to Contemporary Liturgical Renewal" (Ph.D. diss., Emory University, 1988), 114–15.

that our embodied reality and gospel have much to say to each other. Gospel still stands outside our door, waiting for us to let it in so that it might invite us to dance.

What would a truly kinesthetic homiletical process look like? Before we explore that question, it is pertinent to note that this will not be an undisciplined approach. We are not looking here for random movements that might possibly represent something in the text. We are first of all subjecting ourselves to the discipline of tuning the "eyes and ears" of the body to the text,[14] setting our musculoskeletal scene in readiness to experience and respond to the movement of the Spirit that enlivens the text.

For many, that discipline may mean reading the text many times in advance so it sinks into our being.[15] Then, sitting on the floor with open space surrounding us, we begin our particular work on the text with deep breathing that allows us to tune out externals, quiet our mind, and tune into our enfleshed reality. We feel the breath move in us, the wax and wane of the diaphragm, the contract-release of the rib cage. Nerves and muscles tingle; we feel the rhythmic pulsing of the circulatory system. Slowly the text rises out of our depths, in words or phrases or even as experiences of feelings or sets of interactions. We attend to what our muscles do in response to any fragment of the text— tighten or relax, perhaps the heart begins to race—and we attend to what the muscles *want* to do. We let the muscles, tendons, and joints move as they will. We invite and encourage them to act on even the most faint and tentative impulse: reaching, curling up, standing, slumping, leaning this way or that, twisting, twitching. We taste each word/ phrase/pericope as kinesthetic reality, staying with each fragment of the text as long as needed so it can address us fully in our embodiment and so that we can physically explore its dimensions.

So, for example, we might begin with a sermon on John 1:1ff. Our initial impression of the passage leads us to sit cross-legged on the floor, hands in the lap, head down, curled in upon ourselves (fig. 1.1A). "In the beginning . . ." Beginning has an opening feel. The body impulse is to straighten—not all at once, but in rhythmic waves. The small of the back pushes in, uncurling the spine and lifting the rib cage just for a

---

14. We note that eyes and ears are more obviously connected to the body than to the mind.
15. One method is to tape-record the text and then listen to it as one moves, but this may short-circuit the kinesthesia if the body-time and the tape-time are not in sync. One needs to give a word or phrase as much time as it requires and not be interrupted by words the body is not yet ready to experience.

moment before it collapses inward again. But "the beginning" has only begun, and so the movement is repeated, this time with the head coming up as well; next time, the shoulders straighten (fig. 1.1B). Already we have discovered that beginning is not a set, singular moment or event in time, but one that grows slowly, rhythmically, outwardly rather than inwardly or linearly, from a solidly grounded center.

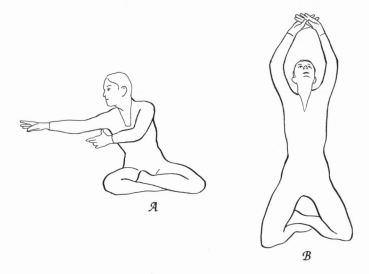

A

B

Fig. 1.1 "In the beginning . . ."

The movement continues with "was the Word." Now with the uncurling and the uplift our arms move out of our lap and to our sides before we again collapse. Opening yet again, the arms now reach back and stretch up to take their place above and just forward of our head. The fingers are spread wide as the hands overlap, palms out (figs. 1.2A, B). The word is found to be multiple, multidirectional, multidimensional, open, active, and thoroughly connected to the centeredness and rhythms of beginning.

Fig. 1.2 ". . . was the Word"

"And the word was with God." The open hands move down, reaching now to the right and pulling the whole torso that way (fig. 1.3A) then to the left. God, we discover, is that which draws us, that which is expansive, embracing all reality, reaching beyond reach. Yet the word is bound to God as firmly as arms are set in shoulders and integrated with toes. "And the word was God"—we are lifted off the floor to our knees, arms rising again into the spread-finger, overlapped-hands form of the word, held, held, held there (fig. 1.3B).

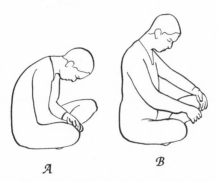

A   *B*

Fig. 1.3 "and the Word was with God"

Here we discover the mystery, the awesomeness of God catching us up and captivating us, until "the word was in the beginning with God" sits us down again, brings those open hands down again, but this time the back remains straight, the head up. The hands are still overlapped and open, but now with the palms in, held at chest level and gently out from the torso (fig. 1.4).

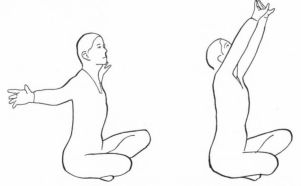

Fig. 1.4 "The Word was in the beginning with God"

Now we understand that the word/God are an integrated whole, yet of distinct manifestation in movement. The word is centered in God and always in dialogue with God. So we move all the way through the text, allowing our body to reveal what our mind might never discover, living the text as fully as we can as human persons.[16]

This is but one choreography by the text—each person who is moved by it will likely move it differently. Every text will move each of us uniquely, as well. Our task is not to design steps for the text, but to be observant of all the tiny feelings and impulses the pericope produces in us. We will also be attentive to moments where nothing seems to be happening at all. Even then we will feel the kinesthesia of breathing and blood flowing, perhaps an almost imperceptible tightness creeping up the neck, or a transitory wrinkling of the nose. We jot these bodily responses down in the same way we would make notes using any other exegetical approach, registering puzzles, problems, and emotional reactions in addition to movements and what they are to us or suggest to us about the text. Doing this work with others expands the possibilities even more, because each person's unique movements will reveal to us something special, in the same way that each mind brings its special perspective and ideas to classical exegesis.

We will want to do such embodied work close to our classic exegetical resources, so words and phrases of dance can be compared with, strengthened, or even redesigned by understandings arising from conventional exegesis and research. But the movement remains the primary medium, aided and supported by the traditional approaches and tools. Not inattentive to what the text or biblical scholars say, we nevertheless focus specifically on what the text does as embodied in our movement. Thus we discover, for example, the possibility that rather than talking about doctrines of preexistence, divinity, and otherness of Jesus the Christ, John 1 is encompassing and integrating us into God.

Kinesthetic homiletics aims at clarity in bones and tendons flexed and released as well as clarity in concept of what this text is as lived experience. When we have done our work well, this clarity can be expressed concisely in simple phrases of words and movement. Such phrases reveal what this text can do with this people; they present in capsule form an integrated, real moment of life lived with God and others. Then we move on to questions of what we might and will do and how we might and will do it in this sermon-to-be.

---

16. Nor can we ever know what is being revealed to us entirely anew, and what we have already known but are now putting to movement. But the same is true of more conventional processes, despite encouragement to be conscious of what we bring to a given text.

The actual shape of the sermon may be derived from the movements we have already experienced. We may rehearse them one by one, now asking what they tell us about the overall form of the sermon and its particular structure. What patterns do we experience? What rhythms? Is this a percussive sermon or a sustained one? Are its movements small or exaggerated? Does the energy grow from a still, small voice to a raging tempest, or the reverse—or does it move in waves?

So also we will ask about the relationships between our movements and movement sequences and the embodiment of ordinary life, our own and that of our people. Is the pattern embodied by this text that of startling awake to the alarm, reaching out to shut it off, rolling out of bed, and stumbling to the shower to be straightened up there, only to sit down again for breakfast or in the car? How is the word multiple in character and overlapping for our people? Is it spoken in greeting and sermon and business meeting? Is it tasted and smelled in communion and potluck supper? Is it opening, challenging, and pulling them this way and that as they balance responsibility toward family with responsibility toward the world? Are any of these movements echoed or parodied by our daily activities? Do we stretch and reach to give, or to receive?

Perhaps we will simply dance the sermon as we have danced the text, although that is not necessarily our goal. Or possibly the outcome will be some combination of spoken presentation and dance presentation, the permutations of which are numerous. In all likelihood the sermon will shape itself as a more traditional aural/oral event, yet it will be preached as well as experienced by the congregation out of the event and impact of the embodied process. A preacher whose whole reality has been rearranged by the phenomenon of embodying gospel must surely come into the congregation with something more than words about the text. So the whole sermon will be different from one conceived in the head, and it will look and feel different to both preacher and people in the pew. It will be gospel bodied forth in the midst of the congregation, gospel that meets and relates with the community not as message but as lived experience.

We cannot yet know where this homiletic might go, for we have only touched one verse and in no particular community context. But we have done enough, I hope, to suggest that the possibilities are both endless and exciting, and to challenge us to take our bodies seriously as instruments and vehicles of the homiletic enterprise.

We can adopt a kinesthetic homiletic without learning a particular dance discipline. The benefit of such learning, however, is the assistance it provides in the process of discovery. Modern dance has particular strengths in making evident the power of movement to find and embody meaning, in helping students discover movements that are inherent in the body but have been suppressed by enculturation, and in setting free the imagination in the playground of the body for the purpose of experiencing gospel in a systemic and wholistic way. Because there are no correct movements in modern dance, because body types and shapes are largely irrelevant, because there is no expectation of conformity to an externally determined norm, modern dance has the capacity to both free us from our inhibitions about bodies and movement as well as to provide a healthy discipline for learning to live more fully and joyfully as an embodied individual and in relation with others.

Gospel is acted, not "merely" said. It begins in act (God's), and it is acted out in bodies (ours). Finally homiletic can be nothing other than kinesthesia: movement and the sensory experience it creates, from start to finish. If we do not begin and sustain our homiletical enterprise in mobility, what on earth makes us think people in the pew will end it actively?

2

Embodying Gospel Corporately

Preaching is embodiment of gospel. But gospel does not belong only to the preacher, gospel is not embodied only in the preacher. Gospel belongs to the whole people of God, and so does the homiletical enterprise.

The body, we are told, is the temple of God, and we are called to glorify God with our bodies.[1] Every Christian is a member of the body of Christ, and every Christian is called to manifest gospel. Every Christian is called to live it out in the world in ways that proclaim the love of God for us, that embody God for others, and that invite and empower all people to participate in that love. We have blithely assumed that if people hear the word "rightly preached" they will be able to go out and "proclaim" gospel in the world. Some hearers are able and some do leave church on a Sunday morning to tell and enact good news at work and play, but many other pew-sitters are not enabled. Many do not proclaim gospel, or do so only minimally or indirectly. They may be nice folk, but it is often not apparent that they are anything else or more. Worse, many people no longer are interested in gospel at all, at least not in the church's version and expression of it, either because they do not experience gospel there or because they do not see or believe that it has anything to do with their lives. Preaching for such folk is only so many pious words; creeds and prayers have nothing to do with contemporary reality, to say nothing of baptism and supper.

1. 1 Cor. 6:19; the specific reference is to the Spirit; 1 Cor. 6:20.

My purpose here is not to provide an in-depth analysis of why "mainline" Christianity, if not all Christianity, is a minority religion in the world and struggling for survival. But one claim I do make: As long as pastors do the worship event for the people, as long as liturgical forms are designed and texts produced without the hands-on participation of the folk in the pew, *as long as sermons are created in pastors' heads and without the active involvement of members of the congregation,* the church will be only half as effective in the world as it could be because of its fundamental disconnection with the everyday embodiment of its constituency . . . no matter how many Bibles there are in the pews.

Gospel belongs to the whole people. Gospel is meant to be embodied not just by the preacher but by the entire Christian community. The problem is that doing gospel in our complex world, distant by two thousand years and half a globe from the stuff of Scripture, takes a lot of learning and practice. As long as the pastor hugs the homiletical discipline to his or her chest and creates sermons in the closet, the people in the pew are being cheated of essential skills and exercise needed to equip them for their own evangelical living in the world. If we expect congregation members to live out gospel on the street—to proclaim it clearly in the way they play tennis, work their way through a conflict in the office, ease through a crowded airport—they must have both primary experience and plentiful rehearsing of intersecting contemporary reality with Scripture so that they can put the same skills to work outside the sanctuary doors.[2]

Nor is it adequate to suggest that since liturgy is the work of the people, liturgy suffices to give them enough practice. In the first place, we can surely question to what degree liturgy *is* the work of the people in most churches. More importantly, we cannot separate homiletics and liturgics. These are a whole, even as is body/mind. Moreover, because the sermon is our most intentional presentation of Scripture, and because our concern is precisely that of intersecting Scripture with all of every Christian's life, building sermons needs to be the work of more than just the preacher—it must include the congregation. The homiletical process, no matter how long we have denied it or how hard we continue to try to avoid it, is a group process.[3]

2. I am indebted to John Burkhart for the idea of worship events serving as "dress rehearsals of life lived by the grace of God." John E. Burkhart, *Worship: A Searching Examination of the Liturgical Experience* (Philadelphia: Westminster Press, 1982), 31, 33.

3. For a significant exploration of this group process, see Arthur Van Seters, ed., *Preaching as a Social Act: Theology and Practice* (Nashville: Abingdon Press, 1988).

This means more than that the preacher keeps the text in mind as she or he goes about the weekly visiting; more than that the preacher engages members of the congregation, either individually or in groups, in conversation about the text; more than that the preacher thinks about the congregation while preparing the sermon. Optimally, corporate homiletics means that the pastor works with a group of people from the congregation through the entire homiletical enterprise—from choosing a pericope for a given date/occasion, dialoguing with the text, positing ways of bringing the event of the text to the congregation as a whole, presenting the sermon, assessing it, defining and implementing strategies for the future preaching of the community.[4] Furthermore, because all people are more than minds, our corporate homiletic will engage the people in embodiment, helping them to become with us kinesthetic homileticians for every day of the week.

Early in our lives we lose the ability to move freely and spontaneously. Perhaps this occurs in puberty; the child who scampered every which way without notice of intent or agenda in mind, gleefully rolled down hills for the sheer pleasure of it, jitterbugged to music with no steps anyone had ever before seen, quite unexpectedly seems to become a different body. I remember, as an adolescent, trying to figure out how to walk. Suddenly something was wrong with allowing my body to do what it naturally did—partly because what it now naturally did was vaguely awkward. Being compressed into constricting bras and pinching girdles, stride-shortening tight skirts, and unbalancing high heels did not help. Nor did regular commands from parents not to slouch, or the little pamphlets young women were given about makeup and fashion and how to walk gracefully (did young men receive similar information?). I remember feeling clumsy until my late 20s—not because I was, necessarily, but because I had encountered so much law about how to move one's body that there seemed to be no possibility of moving correctly, let alone freely.

But in fact law was imposed well before adolescence. "Don't run in church." "Walk nicely." "Sit still." "Put your feet flat on the floor" (which

4. Whether or not the preacher uses the lectionary and/or follows the liturgical year affects this process, but it is not of particular concern here.

Such a group might be constituted solely for the purpose of corporate homiletics; it might be a youth group, Bible study group, the church governing body, or a particular family group. Several groups might work coincidentally on different texts or events. Ideally any group would have both continuity and change, so that the group would not grow stagnant, but neither would the preacher continually have to reinvent the wheel. Moreover, such groups could eventually provide every member with opportunity to learn the skills of intersecting Scripture and reality. For further address of this topic, see Don M. Wardlaw, "Preaching as the Interface of Two Social Worlds: The Congregation as Corporate Agent in the Act of Preaching," in Van Seters, *Preaching as a Social Act*, 55ff.

I, being short, could never do without the prohibited slouching). "Don't squirm." In torturous gym classes we learned to hate our bodies for what they were not and could not do. Rather than being given the freedom of our bodies, we were taught how to bludgeon them into order. Part of the fault lay in dualistic theology obsessed with subjugating the body; the body was at best a container for the mind and the soul. True, the body was functional, and we were to keep it fit because it was functional. But the body was always controlled by the mind, never given freedom to be what it is, let alone freedom to shape the mind or the soul. How often do we still hear extolled the virtue of (superior) mind over (inferior, if not villainous) matter?

Nevertheless, in recent years we have begun to recover the value of the body and to live with it as something more than a container. At the very least we recognize that a healthy body can help create a healthy mind and a healthy mind can help create a healthy body—even if we cannot agree what "health" is.[5] We know that if we are sufficiently wounded in spirit, our bodies can become the vehicle of expression of that hurt via an autoimmune disease, stroke, or cancer. Conversely, if our bodies are traumatized enough, our mind/soul can come apart. Many of us jog or ski or trampoline or do weight training because we know that an out-of-condition body can have serious detrimental effects on our entire life.

Yet there is more at stake than getting the body fit and keeping it tuned up so the rest of the self can carry on. People are often amazed when I tell them I race-walk four miles a day, seven days a week, no matter the weather (yea, verily, in minus-40-degree temperatures, or in rain, and in any other climatic inclemency), not only because it is good for me but because I love it. Certainly there are days when I am less than enthusiastic about doing it, and some days I opt to ski or skate instead. Perhaps next year I will find something I love even better. But I walk not because I must just to keep healthy and sane, but because I love race-walking. It feels good and right for my body, my body wants to do it. My inner self delights in the body-work/play, even as the body relishes what the mind can do in its unique arenas. Both aspects need to be celebrated and enjoyed, not just kept functional.

I am not interested in media images of bodily perfection. What does concern me is that we consider our bodies as well as our minds precious,

---

5. See Jürgen Moltmann, *God in Creation: A New Theology of Creation and the Spirit of God* (San Francisco: Harper and Row, 1985). Translated by Margaret Kohl from *Gott in der Schöpfung: Ökologische Schöpfungslehre* (Munich: Christian Kaiser Verlag, 1985), 270–75.

and care for them faithfully and lovingly. Having only one leg or suffering from asthma or arthritis is not at issue here. What is at issue is keeping what we do have in the best possible state so that we can more fully enjoy the gift of embodied living. Unquestionably, keeping a healthy body and a healthy inner being go hand in hand, because they are the "inside" and the "outside" of the same person. We can only benefit from learning anew how to value our bodies and maintain a healthy, balanced relationship of all the various aspects of our being.

How tragic and absurd it is that we have to learn how to do this! How sad that I had to relearn spontaneity and freedom of movement by taking modern-dance classes because early on I was taught *not* to live my body.

All of this makes it plain that bringing movement into homiletics from the inception of the process needs to be learned, because homiletics has for so long been a cerebral process, because we have been taught *not* to process theology through our bodies, and because we have lost the ability to move spontaneously, to be fully embodied.

The process of learning how to embody homiletics may be different from the process ultimately employed in embodying homiletics. The brief summary of embodiment reflected in the first chapter is the result of learning. Because I now live my body, because my sensitivity to my body is heightened by formal study, I can turn exegesis over to my body, attending to its movement desires—as opposed to sculpting my body in the shape of a vision the text creates for me. I can do this because I know that my physique, my intellect, and my imagination will work together responsibly at the behest of the text and through the power of the spirit. But because most of us have not yet reached this point, because most of us are inhibited and embarrassed by our body as a medium of expression, we begin not by letting the body be but by training it—and therefore freeing it—to do what it ought to do naturally and will do naturally again, given time and practice.

Embodying homiletics consists in three fundamental aspects: (1) Becoming conscious of what one's body now does. (2) Learning the movement possibilities of one's body. (3) Integrating movement and text. The intent is to keep the three aspects together, since what we are after in the end is an interwoven whole rather than parallels, poles, or pigeonholes. But as in all learning, sometimes the focus will be on one dimension more than on another. Because we begin where bodies are, and because we want to initiate as well as sustain the homiletic enterprise with embodied movement, we start with movement conjoined with text.

This process requires only one thing; dance training is not it, although that can be helpful. The requirement is willingness to risk. After all these years of being kept under tight control, we may discover our bodies have some surprising, and perhaps embarrassing or painful, things to say to us. At times we may feel stupid or inept or, as we did in adolescence, just plain clumsy and awkward. Therefore, we will be careful to unwrap and display at the outset one of the gifts of modern dance training: the idea, lived out in experience, that *there are no wrong movements*.

Yes, movements exist that do not belong to a particular body right now (or perhaps ever), and we can create movements that may lead to injury. Additionally, certain movements may express a thing more effectively than other movements do—a definitively pointed finger enables us to see exactly where we are to go far better than does a vague nod of the head. The question is, does this particular movement do what this body wants? Does it do what the text wants? Are the desires the same? If not, which movement shall we choose to attend to? The enabler of any group of budding embodied homileticians will find it essential to remind the group repeatedly that movement in the preaching enterprise strives to be nonjudgmental.[6] No movements are right or wrong in themselves. Indeed, we can learn a great deal about ourselves, about movement, about a text, by inadvertently tripping over our own feet and collapsing in a jumble on the floor. Moreover, the aim of kinesthetic homiletics is not to create dancers for the sake of the dance, but to empower homileticians to embody gospel—and gospel is nothing if not sufficiently grace-filled to make up for what we lack.

Naturally we may discover a thousand other excuses why this cannot be done, besides our disquiet about the body. Homiletics as a group process, and a kinesthetic one, stands against all sorts of patriarchal notions that we treasure—including the already noted dualism that separates mind from body, elevates mind and is embarrassed about the body. Other unhelpful notions include intellectualism that claims that gospel is an idea, a truth; classism and clericalism that insist the pastor's job is to preach in church, explaining to the people how they are to live their lives, while the people's job is to do what the pastor suggests; ageism and able-ism that tells us babies and old people and people who move via wheelchairs cannot possibly dance; and so on.

6. For an exposition of this idea with regard to liturgical dance, see Lu Bellamak, *Non-Judgmental Sacred Dance: Simple Ways to Pray through Dance* (Austin: The Sharing Company, 1978).

The fact is, gospel is wholly inclusive. Every body is part of the body of Christ and the temple of the Spirit. Nothing—not human traditions, rules, or expectations, not two left feet, not arthritis or even quadriplegia—can stop the healing and life-giving movement of the Spirit through us if we let our fears and our expectations evaporate under the influence of the divine *ruach*. Finally, is not the task of the pastor to work with the community so that each of us can be freed from the obstacles we create and the walls we build against God and each other, and fully engage in multidimensional, mutual relationship with God and one another, and so become what we claim we are: the *body* of Christ? Homiletics has to do with enabling people to live in gospel relationship, embodied relationship. Preaching is communal dance.

What process will accomplish this goal? Where do we begin? Not with rules, clear-cut definitions, or footsteps painted as a map on the floor. We begin with ambiguity: recognizing that there is no one right way, no fail-safe pattern, no definitive form, no perfect pedagogy. Homiletics, like gospel, is inclusive, eclectic, contextual. It depends on the uniqueness of the text, on the unpredictable movement of the spirit, on the imagination of the preacher and the people, on the available space, time, energy, courage. The design presented here is a proposal, one that works in the classroom, and one that also can be adapted to other settings as need and opportunity allow.

Academic training and anxiety about shortage of time gear preachers to open the Bible to the given text and plunge in, becoming operators on it—surgeons, if you will, dissecting it and stitching it back up again with the aid of favorite commentaries, and maybe the newspaper or a recent movie as a guidebook. We already know the fallacy here: that Scripture is object. Quite the contrary, if we take seriously the faith claim that Scripture is *living* word/act—a word that addresses us, an act that invites us into itself—we accept the text as subject and we become not objects but participants in a relationship initiated by God, who, through Scripture and the work of the Spirit, embraces us by giving the divine self to us and enabling us to respond. So we begin, ironically, not with activity, mental or physical, on the text, not by diving into the text, but with sinking into ourselves, flowing into the center of our being, locating ourselves in our ultimate reality.

Away from jangling telephones and other intrusions, we get into a comfortable position, in a chair or on the floor, sitting or prone, so that the body is fully supported and needs expend as little energy as possible in keeping itself in place. We close our eyes and take a deep, long, slow breath in . . . and release.[7] Breathe in . . . and release. We repeat this, following the breath with the eye of the mind, each time breathing deeper and deeper, until the breath swirls from the top of our head down to the tips of our toes. With each breath, our body/mind relaxes, and in time we let the breathing bring us to the center of our very being. We float there, sustained by the breathing. As we float, we gently become aware that the center of our being is the presence of God, that we drift in the warmth and light of the very heart of God. We are home, calm, open, waiting . . . When we are ready, we "come back to the room," and open our eyes.

This centering experience takes only a few minutes. Some find it strange at first, and some resist it or struggle with it. Yet it is, in the final analysis, prayer. It can quickly become a gift that equips us like nothing else to participate in Scripture. It reveals us to be integrated beings; it consciously connects mind with body and the whole person to the One in whom we live and move and have our being (Acts 17:28).

The next step is to look at the text for the given day.[8] We read the text silently, then aloud together. We talk about how it reads differently aloud, as it is voiced by our mouths and heard by the outer ear as well as the inner one (if there were no difference, we could simply hand out a printed text of Scripture and sermon to be read silently by the congregation). This reading needs a chance to percolate within, and so we put the passage away for a time while we work on something unrelated. We do make note of any thoughts we have about the pericope before the next intentional consideration of it.

When we next take up the text (preceded by the centering exercise/prayer), the group again reads it aloud. Next we read it aloud standing on our feet, then walking about. We discover that the text reads differently afoot than it does sitting in a chair, because already we are

7. Already we put to use the fundamental premise of the Martha Graham technique of modern dance: contract/release.

8. This is my classroom process, and it assumes a text has been selected for the class. Yet, the breathing procedure appropriately precedes any address of Scripture, whether by individual or group, whether the intent is simply to choose a series of texts for upcoming worship events or to work on a particular text or texts for a given date. In my introductory class, the students work through the process with a single pericope on which they will all preach. Their second sermon is done with the same process but in small groups, each of which addresses a different text. Advanced classes (of no more than eight students) may work together on two or more passages in a session, with each student finally preaching on one text. This allows students to experience being both preacher and congregation.

To ensure that we are all working with the same material, I present the introductory students with the text, made fully inclusive, and printed out double spaced on the left half of the page. The space on the right-hand side of the page is used for comments, questions, and ideas. Double spacing leaves the individual room to write Greek or Hebrew, or alternate translations, above or below particular words of the text. With all subsequent passages, however, participants are responsible for typing/printing their own texts.

putting together the rhythms and muscles and movements of the body with the pericope. We find ourselves pausing, in sentence and walk, in different places than we did when we read the text silently, or aloud but sitting or standing. We realize that we want to emphasize different words now, and that our body hungers to move in coherence with the passage. Awkwardness is apparent, however; none of this feels quite comfortable. But it only feels strange, not wrong, so we move on.

Now the text is read aloud by two or three different people. Then another pair or group reads it antiphonally or according to characters. At every step of the process, we ask what we notice that we had not before. "When someone else reads Mary or Peter or Jesus, it feels different than when I do." On further reflection, we find that the emphasis one person puts on a word or phrase can change the whole meaning. We also notice what is absent: "The passage says rejoice! But this time I didn't hear any rejoicing."

Next, participants are invited to stand in front of the class to read, and new discoveries are made. One group member is quite unexpressive physically. Another uses a simple gesture or two, and a third is animated and dramatic. The responses are enthusiastic: "The gesture she made when she read that gave me a whole new idea of what this text is about." "These verses came alive for me—I could see it happening in front of my own eyes." "I found myself in the middle of this event—in the middle of the crowd on the plain, straining to hear Jesus over the noise." "Every time I've read this text I've identified with Moses, but suddenly I discovered I was Aaron!" We make notes of our discoveries. Then we turn to other matters to let this experience simmer a while on the back of the personal "stove."[9]

The whole process is all so simple and obvious, it seems almost ludicrous to bother to put it in print. But what is truly ludicrous—no, tragic—is when the pastor thinks, "I guess I'd better get started on Sunday's sermon," and takes the Bible out and reads silently and starts jotting down notes and consulting commentaries without ever hearing the words with her ears or getting out from behind the desk to feel them with her feet. How on earth can we ever understand gospel as *event*, let alone event of *relationship*, if we never give ourselves the

9. Because this kinesthetic process is new, and because of time and space limitations, this has been the extent of the emphasis on movement in my introductory course. My Preaching Practicum students follow the entire process outlined in this chapter. Their first sermon, however, is created in group process, but without movement. This enables them to build a trusting community that will give them the freedom to "make fools of themselves." The first sermon also provides them with a measuring stick to help them see the difference between sermons prepared kinesthetically and those done in a more conventional way.

opportunity to experience it that way? No doubt we will find it far easier to do this at home or in the study when no one is watching us make fools of ourselves trying to be three different characters or even a crowd—let alone Balaam's ass (Num. 22). But gospel is not only about comfort, it is about challenge, even risk. If we cannot work out a text in public, dare we think we can preach? The gospel scandalizes us, and we are called to be fools for Christ. Moreover, our theology insists on being incarnational and relational. Then what sense does it make to try to proclaim/embody in public what we have not experienced in public?[10]

The next session commences again with the centering process. We are working with Matthew 6:1-21: the proud prayer, the ostentatious tither, the earthly treasures piled up and amounting to rust and ashes, the left and right hands, washing one's face, praying in a closet. I ask group members to dramatize as they read. Each person takes a fragment of the text. Some are quite unable to dramatize it, others offer only the simplest hand movements. Discouraged, a few suggest we should perhaps leave this movement business to those to whom acting comes naturally. But our purpose does not concern acting, and lack of talent is not the problem.

I invite the group to enter a different door: I will read the pericope slowly while the others close their eyes and watch the visions that unfold on their inner movie screen. After a brief silence I ask, "What did you see?" The group reveals they have seen many different images. We write their visions down, on the board, in our notes. The next question is, "Can you move that?" The response is another attempt to describe the scene. But description will not suffice. If we are to be kinesthetic homileticians, if we are to be faithful to gospel, we need to experience these visions, feel them, warm the body by them. So I ask, "Can you wrap this around your body and move it? If not, is there anything in this text—a word, a phrase, a concept, an emotion—that you can move for us?"

Yes. One courageous individual takes the risk, then another, until finally everyone gets activated, including me.[11] Someone opens a closet door and closes it. Another walks around the room boldly, arrogantly, then quietly, furtively. Another hides the left hand from the right—and

10. Some participants, shy in the group, find they can practice and build confidence by working with one or two friends or inviting their families to "play" with the text with them.
11. Occasionally the group leader or enabler has to go first, to give the rest of the participants the idea, and to let them know they are not being asked to do anything the enabler would not do.

laughs at the triteness of it. Someone scrubs her face, dripping water and toweling off, and puts up her hair. I shovel wheat into a pile and collapse as the recognition hits that it has no value—the market is flooded. We find it easiest to begin with logosomatic words,[12] but moods, personalities, colors, implicit as well as explicit, are likely to follow spontaneously or to begin to flow at a prompt. Everything gets noted. Then we go home, astonished that homiletics could be like this, that this experience will better enable our preaching. So far I am the only real believer, but the whole group is beginning to get on board.

We move on to the next pericope, 1 John 3:18-24: "Little children, let us love, not in word or speech, but in truth and action. . . ." What an appropriate text for us, yet it seems to be a more difficult one, for it does not appear to be as full of logosomatic language and vivid images as the first. We locate ourselves in prayer with deep breathing, with a reading of the passage with eyes closed, and with naming the images that do indeed flow. One person envisions a courtroom scene, where the heart accuses and God judges. Another sees an image of children playing happily and freely in a playground and sometimes coming to cling for a spell to the leg of their parent. In another scene a tiny tot, just learning to walk, is held up by its hands by grownups. Sometimes the toddler walks on air, but mostly on the ground. In still another image, a couple amble arm in arm on a beach, laughing and looking at each other, at the sand, at each other, at the sea, at each other . . . I see myself at home, surrounded by my plants and teddy bears, infused with the comfort and the safety of that space. With these images named and noted, we begin to move, each person offering her or his interpretation of one or another of these action scenes.

The idea of children amidst adults twigs the imagination of several participants. But it is hard to be both child and adult at the same time. Suddenly, individual movements get choreographed on three bodies: one "adult" sits on the floor with two "children." One child is huddled, risking only an occasional sideways look at the adult—Guilt Incarnate. The second child is busy communing with the adult, exchanging smiles and little pats, until she sees her sibling huddling. She scooches over, puts her arm around the distressed child, smiles questioningly up at the parent. The parent reaches for the huddled/hugged child, comforts the

---

12. A logosomatic word is one that "proceeds from the creative ordering power of reality, the *logos*, as it works in and through our bodily (*somatic*) existence." Examples include words that indicate movement of the body, such as "come," "kneel," "bow." Troeger, *Imagining*, 55ff.

child, until all three are happy again. A second image is choreographed: a child sits on the floor, glowering up at the two adults who stand on either side. Slowly, one adult's hand reaches down; the child eyes it suspiciously. Then the second adult's hand reaches down. The child suddenly grabs on to each, is pulled to stand tall: we see now three comrades held in loving unity with arms about each other's shoulders. We try out other scenes, other movement experiments. When we stop to think about it, we realize that all language is logosomatic if we but let our imaginations carry us.

What will we do with these images, these movements? Perhaps, in themselves, nothing. But it is now certain that the texts are no longer simply words, ideas. They are intimately connected to experiences, feelings, full embodiment—they are kinesthesia. We can no longer deal with Scripture only with the left brain, nor produce sermons that speak only to the mind. These movements will not allow us to forget them; they have left a unique impression in the middle of our being. What does it mean to love one another? It means going around the room giving gifts to one another—to one a Bible, to another (who has been sneezing all during class) a tissue; a third gets her feet put up; another is hugged. What does it mean to love one another? It means gathering the class in a circle to rub one another's backs, and laughing and wondering out loud what people would think if they happened to peer through the little square of glass in the door. Little children, love one another.

Outside of our sessions the participants will push these explorations further. They will ask every question they can think of about the text, check the Greek, do word studies, research the historical and literary contexts, consider the liturgical setting for the sermon. Commentaries are a last resort—they too easily stifle the imagination and add a voice ignorant of the intersection of the text and *this* reality. Preachers do well to leave commentaries only for questions that their own work has not been able to answer and perhaps as a reality test.

In the next session, when I ask the group what our verses are saying, the answer is an imperative: "Love one another as Jesus commanded." But when I ask what the text is doing, what *we* have been doing, the response is quite different: "Because God has entered into our lives in love, we can enter into others' lives in love." Immediately we see the difference between preaching law and gospel. Instead of a mandate with its implicit accusation, we get assurance and empowerment. Do we simply tell our people that? Not at all. How did we get to this reality? By embodying the text. So, if we are to embody gospel, we will provide an experience of gospel for our people that is created, designed, shaped by our kinesthetic homiletical work.

How do we do that? What shape might this sermon take if it is to effect this experience? What does this sermon look like afoot? If we take our "doing" statement and embody it as a whole, what does it look like, feel like? One person links together previous movements into a flowing chain of events. Another uses some old and some new embodiments. He hammers himself on the head in self-condemnation, hammers himself to his knees and to the floor, ending with a *mea culpa* chest-beating. We are surrounded by stillness. Then we see an ear cock, an opening up of the body, a surprised smile on an uplifting face, a rising. He stands in a wide-open posture with arms stretched out to say "yes!" From there he brings a gift to each person present: a thumbs-up, a pat on the back, a blown two-handed kiss. The community dissolves in grins and shouts of affirmation.

Another group member stands looking out the window; reaches her arms wide to receive and hug to herself. Then she turns away, shaking her head in negation and curling into a ball on the floor. "I'm not sharing what I've got," her body asserts. But she soon unwinds, comes alive again, smiles, jumps up and races around like a little kid full of summer joy. Then, one by one, she comes to each of us with a smile and gentle embrace.

We see the forms these sermons can take in the movements made, forms that are shaped by the dance the text creates. But sermons are not just for us, they are for a community. So we ask how these movements are lived out by people in congregations. "If you were to preach this sermon in your congregation, where would you find it already alive in their lives?" "Where do the movements this text has choreographed in you link with those people?" We talk about connections, rehearse movements, embody new ones. Many possibilities exist here, many different ways the text-in-relationship-with-these-people can be embodied. The group disperses to go about the business of final preparations, each pondering what choices to make, how best to bring this sermon to life.

When the group members later preach their sermons in a conventional manner, we see the impact of their movements in their sermons. The sermons are replete with verbal images—visions of the movements explored earlier, or stimulated by those, scenes that show similar movements common to the community's daily life. A young boy is tenderly tucked into bed; a toddler runs up and wraps her arms around the preacher, planting a kiss on her cheek; tears are wiped away. We note a greater attention to the other senses—olfactory, tactile, taste. We feel, taste, smell as well as see and hear gospel. The forms have been shaped by, or at least impacted by, the preparatory choreography created by the text.

These are not only kinesthetic sermons, they are corporate homilies as well. The experiences we shared in the sermon development process are present in these sermons, implicitly or explicitly. The links with congregational reality and experience are in evidence. Gospel is embodied by the preacher because Scripture has been lived out kinesthetically. But gospel is also embodied by the congregation, because we have bodied it into being together.

At the end of our work together one participant wrote: "I noticed that when each one of us moved the texts, our sermons were much more whole than when we did not do this."[13] Another spoke of "the profound efficacy of movement in sermon preparation." Group members were also extremely appreciative of the group process, which built community, encouraged and supported each preacher, and "ensured that each person had a part in each other's sermons." These preachers could see clearly both the need for and the value of this double-dimension process of creating sermons, even as they were well aware that they were still novices at learning how to do this. They were all certain they did not want to go back to creating sermons in a closet again. They also felt that even if they could not find a way to create a group to work with them, they were still far better equipped to shape a corporate, kinesthetic homiletical outcome than they would have been without the group experience of kinesthetic homiletics.

Anyone can do this kind of kinesthetic homiletic with common, everyday movement. It does not require a professor or a class, although doing it without a group is the least satisfactory. Begin with prayer by centering yourself. Then read the text aloud and on your feet. Find the logosomatic words and phrases and try them on. Look for emotions, explicit or implicit. How do you move when you are angry, sad, baffled? Note the colors—does blue walk while yellow bounces? If a sheep suddenly appeared in front of you, what would you do? Shoo it out the door? Grab the phone and call Animal Control? Reach out and feel its wool—springy and full of twigs and burrs—and then rub the lanolin off on your pants leg? What would you do if someone crashed your party and poured perfume on your guest of honor (Matt. 26:6-13; Mark 14:3-9; Luke 7:36-50; John 11:2)? Jump up from the table? Stand there with

13. Each student preached four sermons in class—the first developed with group process but without movement; the remainder with both.

your mouth hanging open or swallowing hard? Dial 911? What does your body want to do when you read a psalm? If you were unable to speak, how would you give this poem to someone else?

Answering or even visualizing the answers in our heads will not suffice. If we are honest about the event-ness of Scripture, the reality of gospel incarnate, we will embody our answers, we will move the images. We will attend to what the movements tell us—about ourselves, about the content, shape, intent, and implications of the text, about the people in our congregation, about how we can bring this gospel alive for the folk in the pews, people who will process with their bodies, for better or worse, what we do with the sermon.

No doubt the experience will feel odd at first. But then, gospel does ask peculiar-seeming things of us from time to time. Each time we are confronted by a text in the process of preparing and preaching a sermon, we are not only presented with the gifts of comfort and healing that gospel provides, we are not only called to bring those gifts living to our congregation. We are also asked to take risks, to put ourselves on the line, to allow ourselves to be pushed to or even beyond our limits, to envision new visions and live new realities so that we and the people in the pew can become what we are all meant to be. In some ways kinesthetic homiletics makes that task easier, because it provides a road map we can follow. But it also makes it harder, because we can no longer keep gospel in our heads. We must let it permeate and suffuse our whole being, shape our very breathing, and thus our lives anew.

3

Exploring Human Movements

Everyday life for most of us is full of movement. We roll over in bed, sit up, swing our feet out and down to the floor, rub our eyes, stretch, push off into our morning workout. We walk or jog or swim, pumping knees, swinging arms, diving and kicking our feet. We reach out for the tap, into the kitchen cabinet, perhaps elevating onto our toes. We upend the coffeepot or tea kettle over our cup, work our jaws over bagel or muffin, swallow as we eye the clock. We bend and stretch to get dressed, kneel to tie our shoes, shrug into a coat or jacket. We pull the door open, pull it shut behind us, slide into the car or swing onto our bicycle. Our legs and arms work as we drive or ride. We climb steps to the office, pivot and dodge in a busy hallway, turn our head to see who is going by our door. We lean against the door frame, step backwards away from the window, lift books and lower them. Our fingers punch keyboards and flip pages, or we thumb through files. We swing golf clubs, kayak paddles, ski poles. We slide into home plate or down water-chutes. We braid our hair, wrap packages, rub wax onto the car, swat annoying insects.

We are a miracle of movement, even when we think we are still. Just by breathing alone, our rib cage expands and contracts, our heart muscles pulse, our intestines ripple. Even as we sit most quietly, our shoulders rise and fall, our eyelids blink, our lips purse, our nose or toes twitch.

All of these are common movements, movements we know well but rarely think of—unless we have worked or played too hard on the weekend so that each move brings pain. These movements are also the movements of kinesthetic homiletics, as well as of modern dance. They can be done by almost anyone, almost anywhere, without any particular training.

For the homiletician, the benefit of the discipline of modern dance is that most of these movements are brought to consciousness, studied, practiced, enlarged or diminished, combined in various patterns, experimented with intentionally. We discover, among other things, that these ordinary, everyday physical exertions that we never think about are not just functional—they can be and are communicative in a wide variety of ways. We already know this, at least in our heads. But in studying a dance discipline we also come to know it in our bodies in ways we never have before.

In addition, a dance discipline teaches us new movements as well as new ways of doing old ones. It exercises muscles. It can help us develop our imagination far beyond what we can do with our heads alone. Moreover, putting dance training together with the homiletical enterprise provides an experience of mind and body working together, with all our attention focused on mind and body together rather than on either one alone. We become, once again or perhaps for the first time, what we are meant to be: integrated beings.

In this chapter and the next we examine a process of kinesthetic homiletics shaped by the discipline of modern dance, aided by the content of my course in Kinesthetic Homiletics.[1] Although I have training in modern dance and have choreographed and danced in the liturgy, lack of similar training and experience on the part of the reader is not an adequate excuse for skipping this chapter. While some of the information here may not be easily accessible to everyone, much of the substance can be helpful to preachers and enablers of the homiletic experience quite apart from technical expertise in dance.

I launch the group not by moving—although that is a tempting approach. Because participants are nervous and do not know what to expect, and because we are in an academic environment where the head

1. I have taught this course in a three-week mini-term, meeting three hours a day, and in a five-day, seven-hour-per-day session that did not include sermon presentation and assessment within the group. While other formats are possible, the three-week pattern has all the advantages of an intensive approach, and quickly gets stiff bodies functioning and keeps them that way throughout the course. Movement is paced slowly at first, and I urge participants to be attentive to what their bodies are telling them and to temper their movement accordingly. Participants have ranged in age from mid-20s to 50-plus grandparents, and to date none has had much previous dance training. I prefer to use a multipurpose room with a tile floor, which is more conducive to movement than carpet. I find it useful to remove most chairs, desks, and tables from the room because we want to free ourselves from the classroom mentality. Most group members find that exercise mats or throw rugs are necessary for floor-work and sitting.

is always addressed and the body rarely, we begin with what by way of style if not content is ordinary and familiar. I introduce the theology of kinesthetic homiletics through a presentation of the material explored in chapter 1. Then we spend time in discussion and group-building. The latter is essential, since group process and the unconventional medium of our work depend on trust and cooperation. In this step, participants introduce themselves, name their reasons for participating, identify particular expectations or hopes, and express any anxieties they may have about the work we will take on together. We play a quick little game that includes movement and physical contact and allows for plenty of laughter.[2]

Then we begin to explore movements. Group members are invited to do any movement they can think of—walking, crawling, skipping, upholstering furniture, digging the garden, or anything else that comes to mind from their repertoire of activity. Then the whole group mimics each movement, sometimes adding variations. So, if one person skips in a circle, the group follows for a couple of turns and then reverses the direction. If hammering a nail is the motion, we hammer at an ordinary pace, then accelerate the tempo to double time or reduce it to slow motion. While it is helpful for the leader to have a few movements in mind, in all likelihood the students will be more than generous with ideas not only for individual movements, but also for modifications. During this process students will probably remark how klutzy they feel, or how graceless they are. Throughout the course, I offer regular reminders that we are not interested in creating a professional dance company, but in learning more about movement and integrating the work of the intellect with the work of the body.

At the second session I give a brief verbal presentation that outlines basic modern dance theory.[3] Dance is defined as the use of energy in

---

2. The game is called rabbit. The group gathers on hands and knees in a close circle, facing one another. Participants are instructed to place their left hand over the right hand of the person to their left. When they have done this, the leader tells the group that before they can play, a question needs to be asked around the circle. If the neighbor to the left does not know the answer, she or he must ask the next individual. The leader asks the person on her/his left, "Do you know how to play rabbit?" Because no one (even those familiar with rabbit respond no) knows the answer the question goes around the circle until it comes back to the leader, who also responds with "No!" Then the leader says, "Well, I guess we can't play rabbit." Obviously rabbit is a nonsense game, and it could undoubtedly be replaced by something similar.

3. The technical material that follows is largely drawn from Lois Ellfeldt, *A Primer for Choreographers* (Palo Alto, Calif.: National Press Books, 1967), 6–18. This book served as a resource for my modern dance training under Chester Hertling. Other useful books on modern dance include: Aileen S. Lockhart and Esther E. Pease, *Modern Dance: Building and Teaching Lessons*, 6th ed. (Dubuque: William C. Brown Company Publishers, 1982); James Penrod and Janice Gudde Plastino, *The Dancer Prepares: Modern Dance for Beginners*, 3d ed. (Mountain View, Calif.: Mayfield Publishing Company, 1990). Both of these volumes include narrative material and helpful diagrams.

space and time. For a dancer, energy has three characteristics: intensity, accent, and quality.

(1) *Intensity* is marked by the spectrum ranging from imperceptible movement to excessive movement. For example, I might wag my finger at you gently but quite visibly, or shake it vigorously, or gesture with almost no movement but with such great tension that you are frightened by me. Intensity is not, then, a matter of the size of the movement as much as it is of depth of feeling.

(2) *Accent* is the same in dance as it is in music. It can be quite regular, like the ticking of a clock and like most rock, folk, and country music. Or it can be irregular, like the movement of a basketball in a game or the opening section of Stravinsky's "Rite of Spring" and much other contemporary music. So, I can chew gum or tap my foot in a steady, evenly spaced pattern, or randomly; I wobble erratically on new in-line skates through my favorite park until I learn the insistent stroke of a speed skater.

(3) Intensity and accent are both related to *quality*, of which there are five categories: swinging, percussive, sustained, suspended, and vibratory. *Swinging* movement is what two children do with their arms when they walk down the street hand in hand, or the way we move when we wield a well-practiced axe in chopping wood. Such movements are bound to the pull of gravity and vary in speed from start to finish. Drummers are *percussionists*, and so are we when we drum our fingers on the table or feel the thump of our adrenaline-stimulated hearts. Percussive movement may become *vibratory*—rapid, insistent, nonstop. We hear vibratory movement in a soprano's sustained high C, see it in the wingbeat of a hummingbird, feel it in the incessant chatter of teeth when the temperature plummets and we are not properly dressed. *Sustained* movement is connected movement. It has no accent and no apparent start or finish, like the hum of a computer or a note held by a stuck organ key. In our fast-paced, rushing-hither-and-yon culture, we are not much given to sustained movements, but flowing rivers are. *Suspended* movement is that of a kite held just so by the combination of wind and fully let out string, or a Baryshnikov leap that hangs almost interminably in the air. Time, gravity, and our breath are on hold just to the point of impossibility.

Rarely will these aspects of quality occur independently. They *will* occur in space. Space has three characteristics: direction, level, and size. Like so many other aspects of our life, we rarely think much about *direction* unless we are lost. But all day long we move toward, away from, into or out of (pulpits!), on a diagonal, in a zigzag or a curve.

Even these have variations—a zigzag can be at right or acute angles, a curve can become a scallop, circle, or figure eight. What directions do you go in moving around your house? In the chancel? We may be less inclined to use all the *levels* of space available to us unless we have small children. Most of the time we either stand or sit, but in fact we can move while lying or sitting on the floor, in a crouch or on our knees. We may rise to tiptoe (relevé) if we get up in the middle of the night and want to avoid waking the family, or when we need to reach something on a high shelf. As dancers, we also learn to plié.[4] Finally, with a leap or a jump or a springy bounce up the stairs, we find ourselves moving up in the air. These movements can be any *size* from minute to enormous, depending on what we are feeling and communicating.

Time is equally familiar to us, although unless we are musicians we tend to think of time as quantitative—the clock reads 3:45 P.M., we need to be in a meeting in 15 minutes, there is not enough time in the day/week/month to do what has to be done. Time in the world of music and movement explicitly names these characteristics: *tempo*, the pace of movement (faster than a speeding train, slower than molasses in January); and *rhythm*, the grouping of patterns of accent and nonaccent. We hear rhythm in iambic pentameter or a bossa nova, we see it and feel it in the three-quarter time of the waltz or the Fourth of July march. Rhythm reveals itself in the way we brush our teeth, wash our car, or rake the leaves. We cannot get away from rhythm; without it life would be monotony.

Dance also has content, form, technique, projection. *Content* is the meaning, the essence, the subject. This may be implicit in the movement or explicit; it may be a concept, a narrative, or an emotion. We might dance the story of the annunciation, or dance a pattern of startlement, fear, reassurance, denial, puzzlement, anxiety, affirmation. In many cases our movement will be a combination of elements. The way we put ideas or mood patterns together constitutes the *form*.[5] The form could be a narrative plot,[6] the pattern of the beatitudes, an experience of

---

4. A relevé is really "half-toe." The foot bends at the ball, and the toes are firmly on the floor while the heel is elevated as far from the floor as we can get it. Women of the ballet, on the other hand, dance on point, or full toe, with the aid of special toe shoes. A plié is a bending of the hips and the knees, done with the back straight (perpendicular to the floor) and with the feet turned out. The knees are always over the toes. I use only demi-pliés—performed without lifting the heels from the floor.

5. Ellfeldt, *Primer*, 23.

6. See, for example, Eugene Lowry, *The Homiletical Plot: The Sermon as Narrative Art Form* (Atlanta: John Knox Press, 1980). Lowry's students have named the movements of this form as Oops, Ugh, Aha, Whee, and Yeah (25). These characterizations of plot are danceable quite apart from any story content they might contain.

anguish followed by one of freedom, or any number of other arrangements.

Technique in any activity, as well as in dance, has to do with the skill with which we use our resources to attend to details.[7] Do we clearly articulate our words, or do we mumble, swallow the ends of our sentences, fall prey to malapropism? Do we swoop from note to note, sing flat or sharp, or nail each pitch precisely? "Pick up your feet when you walk!" Who of us did not hear that while growing up? Are synchronous movements really synchronous, or is one a weak parody of the other? Indeed, there may be times in kinesthetic homiletics when we *want* to shuffle our feet, when we *want* one movement to be but a mere shadow of another. One of the facts dance recognizes is that energy will keep moving; the only uncertainty is in what direction. The question is whether we are doing what we intend to do, and whether we are intentional about what we are doing.

Preachers should need little definition of *projection*, which is the matter of making ourselves present to our people, of connecting with them, of drawing them into the preaching event.[8] We do this with eye contact and gesture, with tone of voice and the way we dress. In fact, projection is the result of the totality of our being in the midst of the community. We know how easily a misplaced gesture can give the lie to the words we speak or the emotion we express. Our movements can gather people up or shut them out, they can frighten or soothe or challenge. Nor are we in total control here. Our congregations will choose for themselves finally whether they will respond or not to the promptings of the spirit, whether they find us false or true prophets. In the end, a kinesthetic homiletic is grounded by the same bottom line as any other homiletic: giving all that we have for the sake of gospel, we are nevertheless utterly dependent on the movement of the spirit in us and in those with whom we preach.

For that reason modern dance is perfect for a kinesthetic homiletic. It has no set forms, no unbreakable rules, no limits except those of our bodies and our imaginations. Like God, modern dance will not be put in a box, and just when we think we know what it is we discover something quite unexpected that makes us start moving and thinking in new directions, on new levels. Six persons dancing a text will invariably dance it differently, just as they will come up with at least six different ways of wording its essence and six totally different sermons.

7. Ellfeldt, *Primer*, 24–25.
8. See also Ellfeldt, *Primer*, 25–26.

Moreover, a year or three years from now, when the same six preachers are choreographed by the same pericope in a different community, the dance, the sermon, the reality will be a new experience. God will not be neatly packaged and tied with a bow; the Spirit will blow where it will, and the faces and physiques of Christ are as many and varied as those of our global population.

Nevertheless, neither modern dance nor homiletics, nor the two woven together into kinesthetic homiletics, will be undisciplined. Standard exercises help us to begin to teach and train the body, to work the imagination, and to expand the resources and abilities of the whole person toward wholeness of being and preaching. These include warm-up exercises, movement across the floor, and improvisation. Warm-up exercises are *axial* movements, as opposed to *locomotor* movements that travel across the floor. Both warm-ups and across-the-floor patterns are conceived of and demonstrated in advance. Improvisations, on the other hand, are created on the spur of the moment by the individual, and may be axial or locomotor. While warm-up exercises tend to be unvarying throughout a course, locomotor patterns range from simple walking to much more complex movements and combinations of movements of varying level, intensity, size, and so forth. Across-the-floor movements and improvisations may be suggested by the text, or by unrelated experiences, images, and ideas. All three elements—warm-up exercises, locomotor movements, and movements created in improvisation—may be used in dialoguing with the text.

In every aspect of movement, the individual must monitor her or his own body response. A well-trained dance teacher, physical education instructor, or physical therapist can provide essential information that can help prevent injury and train muscles properly. Ordinary common sense, however, goes a long way toward the same end. The body will accomplish a great deal by invitation, encouragement, patience, and a modicum of persistence and hard work. One may become tired and achy, but exhaustion or pain are not welcome. Finally, as with any new physical endeavor, each participant takes responsibility for considering her or his state of health and does only what can be reasonably well tolerated.

The warm-up exercises are taught in the second session and are repeated at each meeting thereafter. I also encourage students to do them on days when the group does not meet, and to continue some well-rounded, whole-body exercising regularly after the course is over. Our bodies are our life, whether we preach through them or not. An unfit body will be a detriment not only to our preaching, but to everything else we do as well.

Warm-ups (Axial Movements)

All warm-up movements are gentle and controlled; clothing allows full freedom of movement.

Floor Exercises

Bend and pulse.
Sit with knees bent to the side, soles of the feet together, hands on ankles (fig. 3.1A).

- Bend over and pulse (do not bounce) for count of 4 (fig. 3.1B); straighten to arched back and pulse for count of 4; :‖ (repeat) for 2 sets of 4, 2 sets of 2, 2 sets of 1.

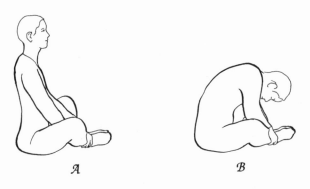

A   B

Fig. 3.1 Bend and pulse

Bend, pulse, and lean.
Straighten legs to the front, :‖ above with hands to front and adding lean to back:

- 2 sets of 4, 2 sets of 2, 2 sets of 1 with first set of each count in point (toes pointed forward as hard as possible) (fig. 3.2A, B, C); second set flex (the reverse of point—the feet bend up at the ankle as hard as possible) (fig. 3.2D).

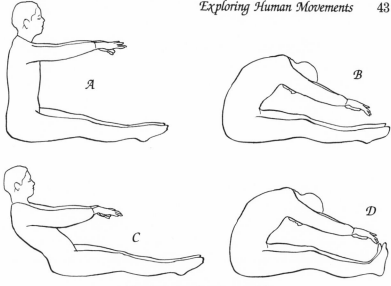

Fig. 3.2 Bend, pulse, and lean

Bend and pulse, second position.

Second position legs (legs spread wide, knees point up, toes pointed), arms reach forward, bend and pulse 4 times (fig. 3.3A); straighten to arched back, arms out to sides, pulse 4 times (fig. 3.3B).

• First set of each count in point, second set flex.

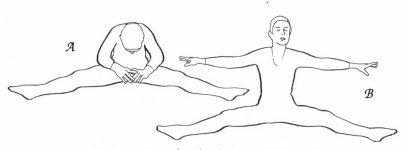

Fig. 3.3 Bend and pulse, second position

Bend, pulse, and sweep.

Second position legs, bend over right and pulse 4 times (fig. 3.4A); sweep the torso and arms over the floor to the left leg, :‖ left; 2 sets of 4, 2 of 2, 2 of 1 (fig. 3.4B, C).

• First set of each count in point, second set flex.

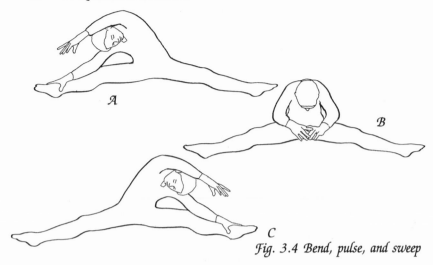

Fig. 3.4 Bend, pulse, and sweep

Flex and point.

Second position legs and arms, arched back.

* Flex both feet, then point, 8 counts; alternating (right foot flexes while left foot points and reverse), 8 counts (fig. 3.5A, B, C).

Fig. 3.5 Flex and point

Side stretch.

Lie on left side, leaning on left elbow and forearm. Bend left knee so thigh is perpendicular to body but leg rests fully on floor.

* Pull right leg to chest while right arm bends behind right hip; extend right leg and arm full length of body 8 times (fig. 3.6A, B), lie on right side and :‖ exercise with left arm and leg.

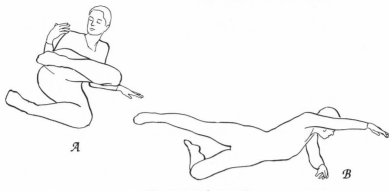

Fig. 3.6 Side stretch

Bend and straighten.

Lie on the back, arms extended to side, legs straight:

- Bring right knee up, toe pointing to floor; straighten knee and extend leg into air; bend knee, toe pointing to floor; straighten leg to floor (fig. 3.7A, B); :‖ left side.

- :‖ sequence, alternating point and flex (on flex, heel touches instead of toe); total of 8.

- :‖ both legs together.

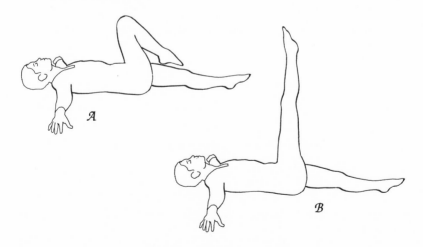

Fig. 3.7 Bend and straighten

Knee and chest.

Lie on back, legs straight, arms extended to sides:

* Bring right knee to chest, raise shoulders from floor and place arms around knee, hold 8 counts, straighten (fig. 3.8). :‖: left leg.

* :‖ sequence, alternating point, flex, 2 each leg.

Fig. 3.8 Knee and chest

Footwork.

Lie on back, legs extended straight up, point:

* Circle right foot clockwise, 8 counts; counterclockwise, 8 counts. :‖ left.

* :‖ both feet, in opposite directions; reverse.

* Feet together point and flex, 8 counts (fig. 3.9A, B).

Fig. 3.9 Footwork

Meet in the middle.

Lie on back, arms extended to sides, feet straight out, point:

• Bend in the middle, bringing arms and feet up to meet in U, hold 8 counts, release; :‖ 2 times (fig. 3.10).

Fig. 3.10 Meet in the middle

Arched sit-up.

Lie on back, arms extended to sides, feet straight out, point:

• Beginning movement in small of back, arch upward into seated position, bending knees as you sit up but leaving arms and head to come up last (fig. 3.11).

Fig. 3.11 Arched sit-up

Graham hip.

Sit, left leg bent to right in front, right leg bent to right on side, arms stretch to right.

• Push right hip up as arms circle left, count of 3; hip drops as arms swing right, count of 3; :‖ one time.

- Hip pushes body to knees, arms arc down in front, then up over head, and down to sit (fig. 3.12).

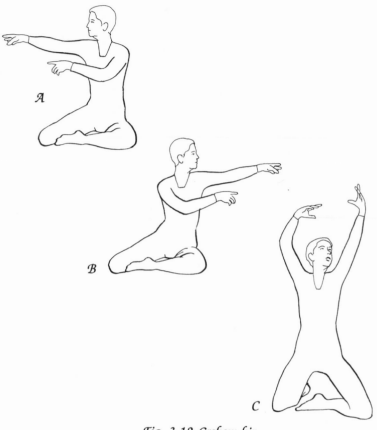

Fig. 3.12 Graham hip

- :‖ previous move, sliding into full-length stretch, whole left side on floor.

- :‖ entire sequence, right side.

Thigh raise.

Sit in a kneeling position, arms down at sides:

- Lean back, pull body to knees through thighs, bring arms back, up, and over head and down to sides (fig. 3.13), sit.

Fig. 3.13 Thigh raise

Dancer's stand and sit.

Sit with left knee bent to right, flat on floor in front of body, left heel touching right hip; bend right knee up and over left knee with right foot flat on floor, hands flat on floor on either side. Push to stand (fig. 3.14A, B).

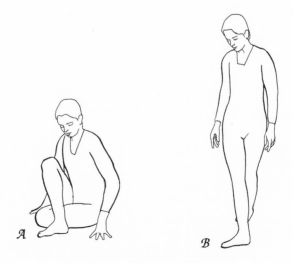

Fig. 3.14 Dancer's stand and sit

- :‖ alternate sides to acquire balanced skill.

- The dancer's sit just reverses this pattern. Place one leg behind the other, toes curled under and *top* of the foot on the floor. Sit by sliding knee down to ankle of front leg.

Standing Exercises

Circles.

Second position (feet shoulder-width apart, feet and knees turned out), hands on hips:

- Roll head down right to left, then reverse (do *not* roll head back), count of 4.

- Roll torso down and to left, right (hands remain on hips).

- Roll torso, with arms inscribing a complete circle, down, left, up (fig. 3.15A, B); reverse, 2 times.

- With slightly bent knees (demi-plié—keep knees over toes and heels flat on floor) :‖ previous step (fig. 3.15A). Also see note 4.

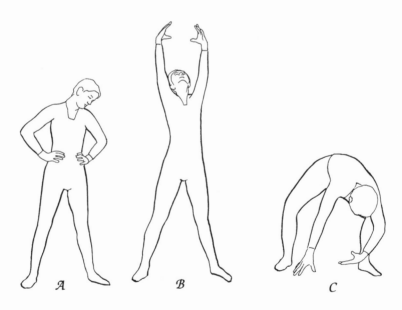

Fig. 3.15 Circles

Bends.

Second position:

- From waist, bend over to floor, pulse 4 times.

- Straighten to flat back (right angle rather than ∩), arms stretched out to sides, pulse 4 times.

- Straighten to erect, arms out to sides, bend left, pulse 4 times; ‖ right (fig. 3.16A, B, C).

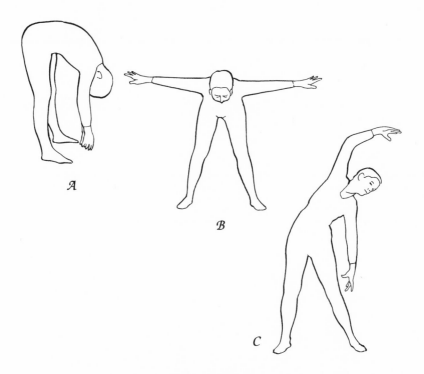

Fig. 3.16 Bends

- Straighten, bend back, arms back, pulse 4 times.

Plié and relevé.

Second position, straight back, arms out to sides:

- Demi-plié, palms down, 2 counts; relevé (up on half-toes—foot bends at ball), 2 counts (fig. 3.17A, B).

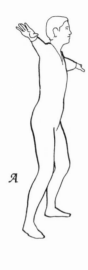

A

B

Fig. 3.17 Plié and relevé

Six positions.

- ꞉‖ in remaining five positions, adjusting arms in positions 3, 4, 5, and 6, be sure to switch feet and arms so both feet get a chance to be best foot forward (fig. 3.18A–F)!

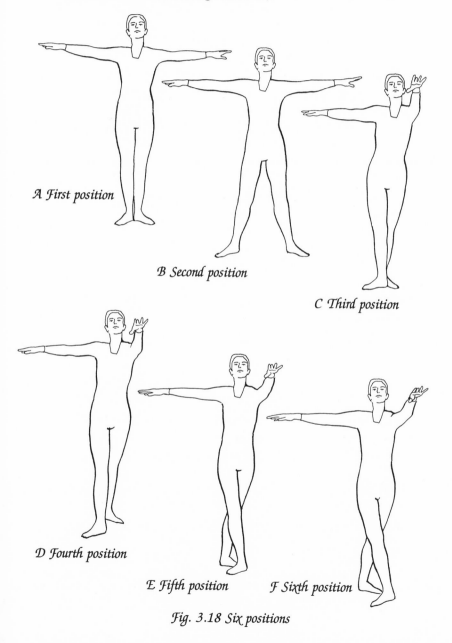

A *First position*

B *Second position*

C *Third position*

D *Fourth position*

E *Fifth position*   F *Sixth position*

Fig. 3.18 Six positions

Barre (chair back or wall can replace barre).

First position, left arm out to side, right arm to barre (between waist and shoulder height), weight on right leg; to the side:

- Point: Left foot moves in point to side (knee stays tight) close to right foot, 2 times; :‖ with flex.

- Brush: Left foot brushes out to side and point (tight knee), close, 2 times; :‖ with flex.

- Developé: Left knee bends out to side, drawing pointed foot up right leg to knee, knee straightens leg to side, bends back, returning left foot to right knee, and then to floor, 2 times; :‖ with flex.

- Swing kick: With straight knee, left leg kicks out to side and point, release, 2 times; :‖ with flex.

- :‖ entire sequence to front; on developé, knee and leg come forward.

- :‖ entire sequence to back, left arm front (on developé, knee goes to side, but leg unbends and extends to back) (fig. 3.19A–F).

- :‖ right side.

A Point

B Brush

C Developé

Fig. 3.19 Barre

D Swing kick side

E Swing kick front

F Swing kick back

Leg swings: Swing leg as far forward as possible and directly back as far as possible (knees stay tight), point and flex; both sides.

Contraction.

Feet closed, arms down to sides, contract at waist (as if to catch a beach ball in the stomach) with arms circling out and bending in:

- Release to right side, contract at waist, arms stretch right and left, :‖ left.
- Release to back, contract at waist, arms up back and over.
- Swing down, up, right with step right, swing clockwise, counterclockwise, close left.
- Contract back, release, contract forward, release (with each contraction, exhale; with each release, inhale; also, each contraction is part of one continuous flowing movement) (fig. 3.20A–H).

Contraction with knee: :‖ front contraction, bringing right knee up, pointed toe and hold; :‖ left.

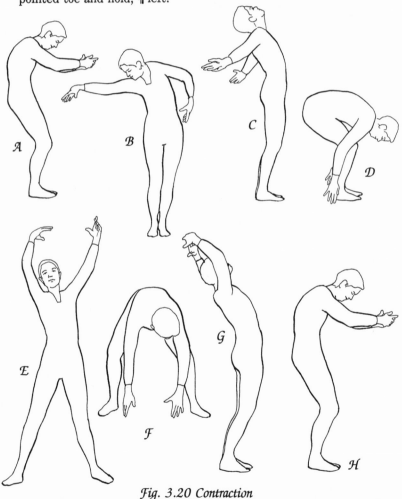

Fig. 3.20 Contraction

Jazz Isolations

These are taught and added to the warm-up routine only after the group is fully familiar with the exercises above. The purpose of the jazz isolations is to separate out particular segments of the body for strengthening and increasing flexibility.

Head

- Keeping face to front, move head right, center, 4 times; :‖ left, front, back.

- Same movement, left, center; right, center; front, center; back, center (or reverse), 4 times (fig. 3.21A).

Shoulder

- Bring right shoulder to earlobe, release, 4 times; :‖ left; then alternate, then both together.

Arm Circles

- With arm hanging, circle right shoulder forward 4 times, back 4 times; :‖ left; then together.

Rib cage

- With hands on hips, face forward, move rib cage right, center, 4 times; :‖ left, front, back.

- Same movement, left, center; right, center; front, center; back, center (or reverse); 4 times.

- Move rib cage in circle, left to right, reverse, 2 times (fig. 3.21B).

Pelvis

- In demi-plié, hands on hips, face forward, move pelvis right, center, 4 times; :‖ left, front, back.

- Same movement, left, center; right, center; front, center; back, center (or reverse), 4 times.

- Move pelvis in circle, left to right, reverse, 2 times (fig. 3.21C).

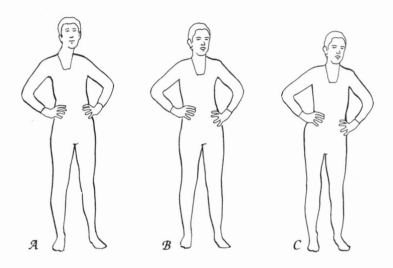

Fig. 3.21 Jazz isolations

Locomotor (Across-the-Floor) Movements

These are taught and used along with improvisations, a few at a time, after the axial exercises are completed. Across-the-floor movements are often done diagonally across a room to make maximum use of space. The teacher or leader demonstrates the movement, and students follow one after the other. Movements can be varied by level, tempo, intensity, quality, size, and direction. Each set of locomotor movements-plus-improvisation which follows concludes successive technique sessions and moves the group into working with the text. Whatever pace of learning of movements is chosen, technique sessions always begin with axial warm-ups, move to locomotor exercises, and finish with improvisations.

Session One

Walk.

- Heel, toe (fast, slow, backward, in a crouch, and so forth).

Ballet walk.

- Toe, heel; with feet and knees turned out, rear toe lightly drags forward into next step; toes are pointed except when foot is flat on floor (fig. 3.22A).

Jazz walk.

- A toe, heel walk with faint resemblance to a stiff-kneed goose step; it is much smoother and gentler than the latter, and smaller (fig. 3.22B).

A Ballet walk   *B Jazz walk*

Fig. 3.22 Ballet walk and jazz walk

Race-walk.

- A heel, toe walk that aims to put each foot down in a straight line with the preceding foot. Each leg swings slightly out to the side as it moves from one step to the next. This generates a lateral movement in the torso that causes the arms to swing.

Triplet.

- First step is down into demi-plié, next two are up in relevé.

- Combinations—Ballet-walk 4 steps, walk 4 steps, triplet 4 steps, and so forth.

- Improvisations (moods): Using any of the above, do a walk that is sad, frightened, dreamy, uncertain, lost, and so forth.[9]

Skip.

- Forward, back, on the diagonal, and so forth.

- Combination with walks—Walk 4 steps, skip 8, jazz-walk 4, and so forth.

- Improvisations (moods)—Do a skip that is excited, painful, lazy, adamant, clumsy, hesitant, confused, and so forth.

Run.

- Heel, toe; toe, heel; in a crouch; on tiptoe; and so forth.

- Combinations—Ballet-walk 4 steps, run 4, jazz-walk 4, skip 4, and so forth.

- Improvisations (moods)—Run in a manner that is wild, somber, bored, relieved, panicky, carefree, and so on.

Additional improvisations for steps in combination: Colors; clock times; newspaper headlines; in the rain; as a serious jogger; suspicious; limping; slow-motion; to a long-lost relative; at the end of the iron-person triathlon; stuck.

---

9. Many of the improvisations come from Ellfeldt, *Primer*, 36–55.

Session Two

Grapevine.

- Facing front but moving to the side, step out right, cross left foot *in front of* right and step, step right; cross left foot behind right and step, and so forth (fig. 3.23A, B); :‖ to the left.

- Combinations—Starting with right foot: walk 4 steps, gravevine 4, walk 4; :‖ starting with the left foot.

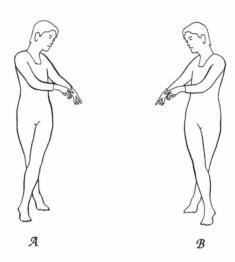

Fig. 3.23 Grapevine

Chassé (slide).

- Facing front but moving to the side, step right, slide left foot to follow; :‖ left; walking or with increased pace and elevation.

- Combinations—Starting right, walk 4 steps, chassé 4, grapevine 4, walk 4; :‖ left.

Lean and lunge.

- Walk 2 steps, on third step, lean forward and hold; :‖ (lean will alternate with left and right foot forward).

- Walk 2 steps, on third step, move weight to front leg with knee bent (foot is turned out, knee stays over toes; back and back leg are straight, heel is off floor), opposite arm comes forward (fig. 3.24A). ⫶.

- Combinations—Chassé 4 steps right, walk 2 and lunge left, walk 2 and lunge right, chassé 4 left; reverse.

Leap.

- Walk 2 steps and leap, repeat; run 4 steps and leap, repeat.

- Combinations—Walk 2 steps and leap, walk 4, chassé 4, ballet-walk 4, chassé 4, walk 2 and leap, and so forth (fig. 3.24B).

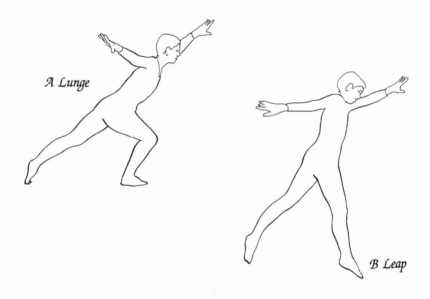

Fig. 3.24 Lunge and leap

Improvisations (direct perceptions).

- Using any of the steps learned, be: a child at play, rocking chair, stormy sea, rush hour, fire, horizon, steaming pie.

Session Three

Rolls (on floor).

- Prone: Stretch arms over head, point toes, roll right 4 times; roll left 4 times.

- Weidman roll: Lie on floor face down, raise right leg, push with right hand and roll to sit, with right knee up, right foot flat on floor, right elbow on right knee; push up off floor with left hand, right arm stretches back over head, left leg straight until body is diagonal to floor (fig. 3.25A, B, C); sit right knee up, right elbow on right knee; roll over left to face down; ⫶ other side.

- Somersault forward, back.

- Use dancer's stand to get up.

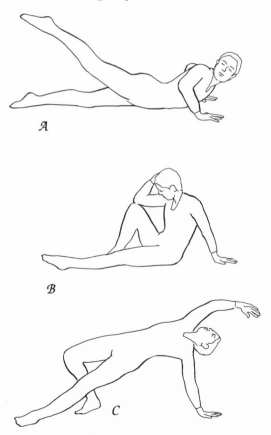

Fig. 3.25 Weidman roll

Turns.

The key to turning without dizziness is spotting. If you are planning to turn to the right, find a spot on the wall in the direction in which you intend to go. Stand sideways to the spot, look right at the spot, and keep your eyes on it until you absolutely must whip the head around right to follow the body. If you are turning left, find a spot on the wall in the direction you intend to go. Stand sideways to it, look left at the spot, and keep your eyes on it until you absolutely must whip the head around left to follow the body.

Three-step turn.

- Right: Stand sideways to your spot, look right, arms at sides. Step out right, arms move out to sides. Bring left foot around forward, bring right foot behind with head (look immediately to spot), step down, slide left foot to close next to right (fig. 3.26A–F). reverse.

- When you have mastered the turn, you can do more repetitions and accelerate the pace, eliminating the close until the last turn.

- Combinations: Walk 4 steps, turn 2, walk 4; chassé 2, turn 4, chassé 2.

Fig. 3.26 Three-step turn

Improvisations (kinesthetic sensations).

- Use any combination of movements learned to suggest: tensing and relaxing; pounding a nail; whipping cream; sailing in strong wind; walking in space; moving on a hot, crowded dance floor; racing to catch a plane; and so forth.

Session Four

Fall.

To prevent injury, falls are done quite slowly. With practice, they can be accelerated.

Begin on the floor with Graham hip (warm-up); do several in both directions.

- Stand, feet together, both arms stretched out to left; swing arms down and around, counterclockwise twice; on second downward swing, bend hips to right, bend knees slowly to bring body to floor; sitting on right hip, and then sliding legs left, arms right into full prone position on right side (fig. 3.27A–D); reverse.

- Use dancer's stand to get up.

Fig. 3.27 Fall

Axial turn.

- Spot! Bring right leg and arm forward across body, then swing right and around, pulling body around on left foot (in demi-plié), step down and close (fig. 3.28A, B). Repeat and reverse. This turn should not move across the floor!

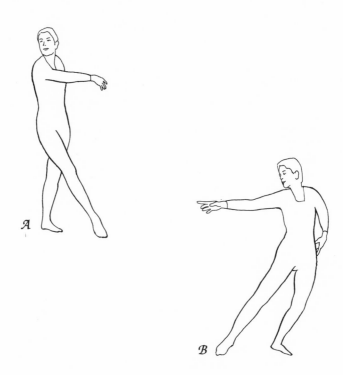

Fig. 3.28 Axial turn

Improvisations (sense memory).

- Use any combination of movements to suggest: being locked in a small, dark room; waiting for someone on a street corner; carrying a great burden; expecting a hot shower and getting a cold one; feeling lost-hungry-scared; cross-country skiing; looking for lost car keys.

Session Five

Kick step.

- Walk with a forward kick.

Pink Panther stride.

- Jazz-walk to the rhythm of the "Pink Panther" theme.

Piqué turn.

- Spot! Step right, relevé on right, bringing left leg into side developé and pivot right, step down left and close (fig. 3.29A, B, C).

Fig. 3.29 Piqué turn

- Combinations—Kick-step 2, piqué turn, kick-step 2, fall.

Improvisations (relationality).

- Relate to: ugly bug, tree, mud puddle, leaf pile, snow drift, wasp, strange noise.

- Warden and convict; parent and child; lawyer and client; pastor and church member; strangers; old friends.

Session Six

Jackknife.

- An exaggerated walk, with knee and opposite elbow meeting across the body with each step (fig. 3.30).

Fig. 3.30 Jackknife

Hip turn.

- Walk 2 steps, step and half pivot (both feet) left to face in opposite direction; step forward to pivot left again and return to original direction (fig. 3.31A, B).

Fig. 3.31 Hip turn

Improvisations.

- Action words: melt, wriggle, ooze, collapse, slink, cling, fry.
- Contrasts: old/young, arrogant/humble, thin/fat, in a crowd/alone, cold/hot, sluggish/energetic.
- Instant images: chocolate chip cookie, crumpled paper, conservative house, growing fern, flashing Christmas tree lights.

Additional improvisations.

Ideas for improvisations are legion, but it is helpful to focus on one particular type at a time. Sources for improvisations can include television commercials, poetry (especially haiku), puns, movie titles, newspaper headlines, and the like. The biblical text may provide all the material needed for improvisations, but because of the participants' sense of reverence for Scripture, secular material may be more helpful in freeing their imagination and movement. Try silly rhymes like the following as an inspiration for improvisations:

- I don't mind eels except as meals.
- Shake and shake the catsup bottle, none will come and then a lot'll.
- At another year I would not boggle, except that when I jog I joggle.
- Spring is here, the grass is ris; I wonder where the flowers is?
- I could of if I would of, but I shouldn't so I douldn't.
- Let us call Yorkshire pudding a fortunate blunder. It's sort of a popover that tripped and popped under.
- I think that I shall never see a billboard lovely as a tree. Indeed, unless the billboards fall, I'll never see a tree at all.
- The pig, if I am not mistaken, supplies us sausage, ham and bacon. Let others say its heart is big, I call it stupid of the pig.

All of this work needs to be spaced to match the abilities of participants. Each session, however, should include some new movement and some improvisation.

Rather than the leader's teaching specific moves, the group can explore movements together. For example, the leader might ask group members what different ways they can think of to turn. Participants could be invited to take this assignment home with them and carefully note down on paper the kinds of turns they do in the kitchen, going out the door, when someone sneaks up behind them and startles them. Then group members can demonstrate these movements in the group session, and each participant can try them. The group can explore how the turn can be done in series, slowed or hurried, or even made better.

Similarly, participants can be invited to find ways of moving across the floor without using their feet, or without traveling in straight lines. How many ways can the group find to move in collectives—pairs, triplets, or even larger clusters? Or, the leader might ask participants to discover examples in their ordinary, everyday movements of vibratory or suspended movements, movements of contrasting speed or intensity, movements that flow naturally from one to another. The possibilities are, for all practical purposes, endless, especially if group members explore ways to change one another's movements—by enlarging or diminishing their size, reversing them, increasing or decreasing their intensity, altering their quality (making a swinging movement percussive, for example), and so on. A video-camera can record movements and they can be studied in slow motion.

Because we are not training professional dancers for the theatre, each session includes work on technique and work on the texts. Dance technique may be the focus of the first half of the session, and work with the pericope the second half, or the two aspects may be more fully integrated.[10] In either case, participants will soon demonstrate increased physical ability and grace, as well as an imagination that grows by leaps and bounds, even as they develop a healthier sense of themselves as whole persons and greater confidence in themselves. Increased comfort in individual and group embodiment experience, along with expanded sensitivity to the way participants relate to energy and space, can significantly enhance anyone's preaching.

10. At the beginning of the course that meets three hours per day, we spend one hour of the daily session on warm-ups, one hour on locomotor movements and improvisations, and one hour with the text. As the course progresses and students acquire experience and confidence, we strike an even balance between technique and homiletical preparation. A similar pattern of balance occurs when alternate time frames are used.

4

Surrendering to the Text

Learning a process of kinesthetic homiletics has involved two broad steps: first, addressing its theology, becoming acquainted with group members, and exploring some basic body movements arising from daily experience; and second, being introduced to basic dance theory and putting this theory into action in the warm-up routine, in exploring across-the-floor movements, and in beginning improvisation.

These physical exertions leave us a little warm, a little out of breath, a little achy. Most participants feel some frustration at what the body resists doing or does not do as well as we would like. We share a good deal of laughter at just how comical our movements can be. Everyone is learning how much our bodies have been neglected, how undisciplined and unskilled they are, how erratic the conversation is between intellect and body when we request specific movements and focus on them. People who have overcome paralysis must surely know about the difficulties of body/mind communication, but we who move mostly by habit have much to learn. We recognize that we are engaged in a process of re-tooling—retooling minds to work in conscious concert with their bodies, and bodies to converse openly and fluently with their minds. At the moment, however, most of us feel discombobulated, disorganized, perhaps even more awkward than we did in our teenage years when (for some, at least) the growth of the bones outstripped that of the muscles, when our legs and arms seemed to have a life of their own. Yet we will not stop here. Now, while we are still very much physically conscious and oriented, it is time to move toward integrating movement and Scripture.

We surrender ourselves to the centering exercise/prayer, breathing in and out deeply, slowly, repeatedly. Group members are directed to find themselves settling into the core of their being, to float there, to discover themselves once again in the presence of God. Compared to the vigor of our early activity, this is a profoundly peaceful moment, a time of fine-tuning our receptivity to the divine impetus. We are in a season of holding ourselves in suspension, an occasion of waiting.

After a time, I read the first passage of Scripture to be addressed: Ezekiel's engagement with the divine *ruach* in the valley of dry bones (Ezek. 37:1-14). This is a particularly vivid pericope, one that readily allows images to flow in the mind's eye, across the internal wide screen. When the participants "come back into the room," they talk about what they have seen. They are impressed by the size of the valley, the glaring, bleaching sun, the arid, dusty smell, the incredible number of bones, the overall grimness of this scene.

I read the text again, this time as the group members walk about the room. As they become engaged in the process of hearing and walking concurrently, some of them are moved to try out gestures or actions. Several appear to be so submerged in hearing the text that they seem to be unaware of what their bodies are doing. For others the embodied response to the words is conscious, self-conscious. One student writes in her journal, "How high would I have jumped if no one had been there to see me? How loudly might I have shouted?"[1] Amid all the evaluation of an academic program and under the influence of a culture that constantly critiques and judges every action, participants find it hard to get free of their inhibitions, even with the daily reminder that there are no wrong movements. The liberation of the body does not happen on command, either our own or another's. It takes time and affirming experiences, and this group has not yet had enough of either.

Still, the kinesthesia of the earlier warm-up and locomotor exercises, of the new movements learned this very day, affects each participant. The working of these bodies has left kinesthetic impressions in each person and kindled their imaginations in new directions. So these preachers try moving some of the images they hold in photographic memory from the first reading. Bit by bit, step by step, they shake themselves free of all those restrictions imposed by "adults" so concerned that children manifest only the most proper behavior; they set aside all the

---

1. Participants are asked to keep a daily journal in which they reflect on each session. At the end of the course, along with presenting a sermon, they write a paper summarizing what they have learned and discussing the impact of the course on them as person and as preacher.

limits defined by a culture that has too long disdained the gifts of the body. A group member later reflects in her journal on the sense of release and play her inner child felt; she ponders whether she is perhaps finally coming to understand something about Jesus' claims that children are the true residents of God's commonwealth.

Eventually, all the participants report they are increasingly aware of movement—their own movement on the street and at home, that of the pelicans bobbing and diving for fish in the river, that of plants moved by wind, that of the wet, clumpy falling of late-April snow. A thawing of muscles and oiling of joints seems to bring with it a shedding of cataracts from the eyes of the inner being as well as of the body.

What does it look like to be moved by God? One participant discovers an insistent attempt to resist—a sharp front contraction in an effort to pull her hand out from the divine hand, a flexed-foot digging in of the heels, turning and trying to run away. Another portrays a surrealistic experience of being gently led in a somnambulist-like ballet walk. What does this valley of bones look like, feel like? One participant gingerly relevés around and over piles of bones. Another descends to the valley floor in a dancer's sit, reaches out, rises in a dancer's stand with a pinch of bone dust that puffs away in the wind when she releases her contracted fingers.

We follow the same procedure with a second text, Romans 15:1-13. This one is not quite as provocative as Ezekiel in its verbal pictures, but the group is not long stymied. We search for the individual words or ideas that can easily be moved. Someone postures a cringing weakling and a muscle-bound weight lifter. Another hugs a colleague in welcome. A third builds up another with pats of affirmation. How do we move insults? Sharp abdominal and side contractions shape this for one person; for another, a fall speaks volumes. What can one do with "whatever was written in former days"? We watch a group member ballet-walk a careful search back and forth along an imaginary bookshelf, then rise in relevé to pull down a volume. He blows the dust off it, opens it, shows it to us with an encouraging, assuring smile. With a sustained circular sweep of his arm, he offers the content to all of us.

For several days we work our way through in this manner, verse by verse, one pericope at a time. Each day, as new dance movements are introduced and become part of the class repertoire, they appear as embodiments of text, tools for discovery and expression of what the words are all about. A series of swinging movements reflects the steadfastness, encouragement, and hope of Romans 15:4. An axial turn becomes the witness of confession, and a series of three-step turns the act of praise. A dancer's stand raises up from the floor the one who will rule the Gentiles. Front contractions enable Ezekiel to be filled with the prophetic word, side contractions breathe it out to transform scattered, desiccated bones into whole persons.

The group explores Scripture with movement, while Scripture explores them the same way—and this in no particular order. At each step discussion occurs. Individual choreographies of a word, phrase, or idea birth affirmation, insight, puzzlement, and even disagreement. This is, after all, a diverse group representing a wide variety of life stories and views. As a result of all these interchanges, movements are modified, sometimes abandoned altogether as connections with the text and among the group deepen and strengthen. Not surprisingly, the participants find they must research some matters in the library. Classical exegetical work done there is later shared in the group, and as a result some movements are reshaped, refined, or reoriented.

Someone soon discovers that the context of the word or phrase being moved suggests a movement for that word different from what the word alone invites. Attending to a word or phrase in context moves us to take on whole verses or even clusters of verses.

All along the way, students spontaneously help strengthen one another's movements and jog one another's imagination. Sometimes a group member will move three-quarters of a verse and say, "I'm stuck. I don't know what to do here." I ask, "What does your body want to do?" More often than not, the response will be a moment of stillness, then a hesitant verbal answer. I offer encouragement to just do the movement and see what happens. In many cases, the problem is solved. If not, I may ask the group, "Who can help us here?" "What if you did this?" someone will offer, and demonstrate. "What if you made the motion more percussive? Bigger? Moved in a circle instead of in a straight line?" Movements and thoughts flow thick and fast. One student, who eventually preaches the Romans passage, writes in her journal, "I am impressed by the idea-building of the group. Even though we see things very differently, the movements build on each other until the pictures and images become motion. What a wonderful picture of the priesthood of all believers in unity!"

The unity is more than that of a group working together to explore movements and build sermons. Day by day the barriers to conversation between cognition and body begin to disappear. The mind soon can say to the body, "Let's do a series of three-step turns to express the movement of the Spirit in the valley of bones," and the body will do exactly that. Similarly, from time to time a participant will get up to move a word or phrase in a certain way, only to discover the body shaping a rather different choreography, one that turns out to be much more expressive than what the mind had planned. Not only has the body begun to trust the directions of the mind, the mind has also begun to be attentive to the body's kinesthesia and to trust that sense to provide essential contributions to the homiletic process. Being moved by the spirit in sustained swings sheds an entirely different light on the text than does being whirled around the room in piqué turns. Becoming a servant through a ballet walk can be an exercise in despair; becoming a servant through a jazz walk is something else again.

Being moved through the texts and moving through them creates in these homileticians an extraordinary awareness of the moods and feelings both buried within and between the words and evoked by them. This is *anamnesis* in the best sense of that word—experiencing the reality of Ezekiel and Paul in our own time and place. We are not trying to re-create those events or pull them from their history into ours; this is not play-acting or bathrobe drama. Rather we are being touched by and touching in our time and space the same reality of the presence and power of God experienced and lived out by the prophet and the apostle, and by all the women and men who people the whole of Scripture and generations of Christian community since the canon was closed.

No traditional word studies, no reading of commentaries, no round of questions asked and answered in the head can have the same impact as the experience of finding yourself heaped on a cold, hard floor, a pile of splintery bones or a helpless weakling; no disembodied search for ideas can equal the event of being lifted up and helped to stand, steadied, and finding yourself reaching out and helping another to rise and become strong. Do you think you know what insults feel like? Try a hard abdominal contraction, or a jackknife. Try them one after the other in rapid succession sufficient to drop you gasping and rolling on the floor. What does it feel like to attempt to save yourself? Let the text provoke you into a series of Weidman rolls—and discover kinesthetically that you never get anywhere, you never make any progress, for all the puffing and sweating you do. No amount of words will tell you this well enough. The plain truth is that if we are to convey these realities to the folk in the nave, we must feel them in our backs, hips, elbows, guts.

"What is the text saying?" is too easy a question. We can answer that out of all the classical exegetical approaches without bothering our bodies, our wholeness, at all. "What is the text *doing?*" Now, that is a different matter. We have the doing in the words on the page, yes. But more importantly, we have it as well in the visions we see of this class member searching the shelves of Romans, or fidgeting on the floor as the dry bones now enfleshed become enlivened by the divine *ruach* inspirated by Ezekiel. Finally, and most importantly, we have it in our kinesthetic memory, in our bones, muscles, tendons, sweat glands, nerve endings, in the sensation of how this reality lives incarnationally. As we read the words anew, the body responds. We feel again the collapse, the uplift, the spinning and leaping we did in praising God. We have all we can do not to succumb again to the same movement. If we have any sense at all we *do* succumb.

But we are not about this business for ourselves. We are here because we are participants in the preaching enterprise. Whatever this text is doing with us, we are called to try to help our community experience what it is doing with them. We need to get some perspective,[2] and so we ask one another more questions. What have we been doing here? What is this Ezekiel passage doing? The text is building up. It is filling and empowering. What is it saying? The spirit of God restores and renews. Through the Spirit we are renewing and restoring. What experience do we hope from this text for our people? Uplift and renewal. Taking in and emptying out. Which of our movements connect with the daily life of members of a congregation?

Group members envision the people of their community, test out the links, the connections, the commonality of experience, and the possibilities for the future. For not only will we embody the text as present to us now, we will also embody its vision for our future life together. In point of fact, these communal questions are not present to us only now. By virtue of including members of the community in the sermon development from the start, these questions are alive throughout the group's work. We ask them here by way of a conscious, intentional review, to ensure as best we can that we have not missed something, to ensure that bridges into the text are as many and as wide and direct as we can build them.

What does this sermon look like and feel like danced? Different experience-generated perspectives of the pericope, preacher, and community shape unique choreographies that map the essential content and the form for each sermon. Preachers rehearse previous movements and create new ones expressive of the whole. They look for and carefully note the patterns, rhythms, qualities of their movement sequence and that of the community.

---

2. Fred Craddock's section on distancing is helpful here. Fred B. Craddock, *Preaching* (Nashville: Abingdon Press, 1985), 117ff.

Of course, not every movement experienced in the kinesthetic sermon preparation is accessed in or applied to the sermon event itself, any more than every piece of data or idea resulting from conventional sermon preparation appears in the homily. Some movements are simply bodily explorations that have no particular lasting value. Others may be catalysts for wholly new kinesthetic realities that spark true embodiments of the text/gospel. As we construct the sermon into its preachable shape, we sift through our entire kinesthetic memory to see what most appropriately and effectively manifests gospel this day. No movement is banished out of hand from our mental or written list of possibilities; each remains a part of our kinesthetic experience and repertoire. Thus all our activity by and about this text becomes a storehouse of treasures that may take an active role in the preaching movement even as we preach. This is so because a sermon is not, finally, a choreographed dance to be performed, no matter how kinesthetically it is created. No sermon becomes a sermon until it occurs in the midst of those with whom we preach. So, for all our intense and careful preparation in advance, we will ever be open to the promptings of the Spirit to move and embody gospel in ways we had not planned. This is a risky business, indeed. But the more we have the text built into us, the more we have lived it, the more likely that our embodiment of it will be authentic and sound.

Group members are free to continue preparing and to present their sermons in any manner they wish. Some finish preparation on their own. Others work together; they may read Scripture for one another, critique movements or verbal content, or take an active role in the sermon itself. They spend time in the sanctuary, testing out how they might put its space together with this text. Suddenly space and its furnishings, while not neglected before, seem terribly important. The radical difference between preaching from a containing, wraparound pulpit and preaching from open chancel steps or wide aisle is only too obvious when preachers have been embodied by their texts through the movement of dance.

The nature of the actual preaching event can range from classic delivery to an unvoiced sermon-in-dance. An about-to-graduate senior knows that few congregations are prepared for sermons that are even slightly unconventional. Yet preaching from the elevated pulpit destroys for him the communal claim of the Romans text, and so he opts to preach from the lectern set down on the chapel floor in close proximity to the congregation. He does not dance the sermon, but his content and gestures are powered by kinesthesia. This is no merely oral/aural event, but one that moves around, through, and with the community, and moves the community.

Another individual believes that opportunity for ultimate creativity will likely be extremely rare in the future—and that is reason enough for preaching with the body, without the voice. We watch this event unfold. Our ears rest in this sermon, but our eyes and kinesthetic memory are incorporated and we are caught up in it as kinesthetic experience. We have come a long way from "hearing" a sermon.

The rest of the group members choose a middle ground, with varying degrees of movement and voice, but full of movement language shaped or inspired in the group kinesthesia.

Presented sermons are videotaped, so each preacher can now see from the outside exactly what she or he did. As we watch, we talk about what we saw/see, how we felt/feel, what we experienced/experience now. We begin with affirmation, identifying what "worked" for us and why. We puzzle together over things that did not "work" for someone, experiment with what we might do differently. We talk about faithfulness to the Scripture passage, responsible address of the contexts of the text and sermon, theological integrity, connection with the whole congregation and their reality, and all the other elements important in assessing a traditional sermon. We pay particular attention to the impact of embodiment and to whether or not gospel is experienced, as opposed to being missing or merely seen or heard.

Comfortable in and trusting of the community built up by this kinesthetic homiletic, these preachers are honest with one another and with themselves. They are relieved and a little giddy, and all feel that they have done some of the most responsible preaching of their lives. They have. The group agrees that this is some of the best preaching they have experienced in a long time. All have experienced gospel in ways they never knew possible.

With perhaps one exception, none of these preachers has become a dancer. Nor is any of these sermons flawless with regard to exegesis, form, trajectory. They vary in viability and quality. Yet each preacher embodies the sermon, embodies gospel, weaves the congregation into the choreography.

Two things are happening here. One is that each preacher is bodying forth a text—we see that this preacher is living this gospel. Gospel is no longer a nice idea, it is made real and present before our very eyes. Nor is it a static truth, for it moves around us, breathes through us and lives in and around us even as it gathers us up into touchable community as the preacher embodies the sermon. The second thing that is happening here is that the congregation has already been—for a long time, in fact—a part of each sermon. Indeed, the congregation has participated in this homiletical event from start to finish. Each pericope is written in our hearts, in our very DNA. We are deeply invested in it, built into it, meeting again an old friend whose influence in our lives has already been profound.[3] We can no more drift off into daydreams or forget this sermon than we can forget to sleep. It will stay with us and empower us precisely because we have not only heard it or seen it, but because we have lived it, at least twice—once in inception and development, and again in presentation.

As this group reflects together on this entire enterprise, we consider that there may be some potential dangers in this experience of kinesthetic homiletics. The first danger is that having lived through this event of gospel, this embodied proclamation, we may no longer be able to endure the ordinary preaching we will surely encounter most of the time (and may even do ourselves). We can only hope that the more kinesthetic the homiletical enterprise becomes, the less focused preaching will be on the abstract other, and the more sermons will connect gospel with our embodied reality and catch us up in experiences that will touch not just our ears and heads but our arteries, bone marrow, and central nervous system. More people will become more practiced at embodying gospel in community and therefore empowered and rehearsed for embodying God in the world. No longer will there be any excuse for preaching disembodied sermons, and those who do will hopefully become a rare species.

A second danger is that such preaching is indeed rich fare, and there can be too much of a good thing. So, while we can and hopefully will be consistent about the discipline of kinesthetic homiletics, the actual sermon development process and preaching event will need as much variety of form, style, and nature of presentation as any collection of more conventionally derived sermons. But this variety will not be difficult to achieve. The more we are embodied by texts and the more we embody them, the more we will be open to the extraordinary richness and diversity of the whole of Scripture. That is not to say that embodiment cannot lead us into ruts. As with any other discipline, kinesthetic homiletics is not something that we learn once for all time and

3. This preaching maximizes re-"cognition," since the community is involved in shaping the whole. But it also manifests newness and discovery, since each preacher finally is responsible for putting the sermon in presentable form. This individual contribution almost guarantees fresh and even surprising content that provides the rest of the community "ahas" and food for further thought/act. See Craddock, 15 and 159ff.

never have to study again. Quite the contrary, it is an ongoing growth process, one that calls us continually to activate our imaginations and challenge our minds and our muscles to new discoveries, understandings, experiences, possibilities.

A third potential danger arises here. "Group process is all well and good," more than one pastor has said, "but when you leave seminary you have to be able to come up with sermons on your own." How easy it is to fall into the old hierarchical, elitist pattern of the pastor as the one who is totally responsible for the ministry to the church! The fact is we can never, if we are faithful to gospel that belongs to the whole people of God, "come up with sermons on our own." Even if, for some obscure reason, we must develop sermons in a closet, we will still invite the congregation in there with us in every way we can. How much more of them can we have with us if we not only know "these" people by the way they think and speak, but also by the way they move, by the way they interact as full persons with Scripture, by the way they embody gospel! Moreover, sermons never come to existence in preparation, they only come into being in the preaching moment, in the midst of embodied persons. They are by default corporate. By involving the community at the start, we are finally getting honest with that truth. Additionally, sermons have a half-life. They are lived out (or not!) by our people after 12:00 noon on Sunday and outside the sanctuary doors. How much more do we reflect these realities, how much more do we embody gospel, when we include embodied persons in the process all the way through!

Yes, we may need to move mountains in order to help the people in the pew into this new world. Yet many of those mountains will be the obstacles we create for ourselves. As for the rest, a mustard grain of faith and our best educational footwork will go a considerable distance toward accomplishing our goal. Undoubtedly some folk will never choose to participate in kinesthetic homiletics, but that must be their choice on the basis of the best foundation we can provide them. Furthermore, if it should come down to a situation where a preacher must prepare in a closet for the preaching event, the closet's narrow confines and silent solitude will surely convict us all the more of the necessity of utilizing every God-given resource we can muster—intellect, imagination, kinesthesia, koinonia.

This kind of sermon development reveals many advantages, both personal and homiletical. Participants report coming to a new or expanded sense of acceptance of their bodies, even though they cannot do every movement, or do each movement gracefully and wonderfully. Even those with physical limitations find this work both strengthens them bodily and increases their flexibility, bringing them to a greater sense of ease about their particular embodiment.

Kinesthetic homiletics becomes, like gospel, an experience of liberation, but also one of integration. Participants relish the blending of body and mind in the proclamation of gospel, they see and feel the necessity of "cultivating the connections" in order to enable the congregation to experience the text coming alive and to participate in gospel. They find that sermons evolve much more easily through kinesthetic homiletics than they do with traditional, intellectually grounded processes because moving through a text brings to the surface insights and images, feelings and experiences buried within and perhaps unaccessible any other way. Being moved by a pericope tends to choreograph a sermon as a coherent whole. Moreover, the language of the sermon is informed by contemporary experience. The preacher is less inclined to archaism or theological jargon, more inclined toward the common tongue, something often hard to come by in preaching despite the insistence of the Reformers and Vatican II. The language is also lively—it dances in front of the eyes, caresses the skin, twitches the nose and toes, releases muscles into rest or contracts them into activity.

With regard to relationships, group-process kinesthetic homileticians experience a new sense of equality in the movement, for neither talent nor expertise is really at issue here. There are no right answers, no wrong movements. The pooling of resources, and the complementing of strengths and weaknesses, lead to increased wholeness in each individual and in community. As trust and community build, participants experience a surrender of the ego that frees the spirit to work, to move, to choreograph, to become embodied in every participant and in the community as a whole. It may be that an individual is the preacher, and he or she is valued for being that. But in fact the whole community preaches, the whole community experiences, rehearses, and lives out gospel.

Yet another benefit is that we can no longer pretend that the written word of the Bible is all there is, God in print. We can no longer treat Hebrew Scriptures as irrelevant or only preparatory. Nor can we continue to believe that incarnation happened only once, back there in Bethlehem and Nazareth when Jesus was conceived and born. When we are embodied by a scriptural passage, when we live it out through group process, we know in our DNA, in the inner workings of our joints, in inhalation/exhalation, that Scripture embodies gospel which is a now interrelationship that depends very much on the persons God addresses participating in that relationship. We find life, grace, gospel in Deuteronomy as well as in Mark. We discover that we incarnate divinity precisely (as we have been told but never really believe) when through our flesh and blood we gift another with comfort, hope, vision, new life. This is a new process, experimental, not yet able to demonstrate the proofs provided by longevity. Who can say where it will lead us? But there are some clues. One participant wrote, "Somehow, it became quite clear to me that God's total creation is a dance, a dance of which we became part. It will be impossible to ever read Scripture again without wanting to move." Another reflects on the experience in kinesthetic homiletics this way: "This has given me a model for ministry. Gospel affirms us, frees us, awakens creativity, and strengthens us so that we are empowered in our service." Would that all our students came away from seminary with this much, would that all the people in the chancel and the pew of a Sunday morning left the sanctuary so reoriented.

Some of these advantages, perhaps all of them, are possible if we work only with "common" movement as opposed to dance movement. But we have seen how the particular discipline of modern dance enables the process. It provides a routine of warm-up exercises that work the entire body and can be learned and done independently any time and any place. Locomotor exercises teach both body and mind about movement in space and add to the repertoire of movements learned in the warm-ups. Both of these foster a new awareness of and intentionality about the body as a medium of feeling, reflecting, understanding, communicating. Improvisations exercise the connection between mind and body in a unique way, putting the imagination to work not just in the mind's eye, but in the whole of the enfleshed person. We rehearse movements in conjunction with ideas and mental images, and we practice the embodiment of ideas and images in giving them movement.

Overall, the technical work provides a structure and discipline that helps us organize the kinesthetic homiletic and maintain a consistency of use. At the same time, the whole person is liberated from inflexible rules and freed to be embodied at whatever level is possible for that individual. We are challenged to experiment, discover, and create out of the treasure house of the fullest possible existence. Modern dance then becomes a gift more than a technique, procedure, or skill. It opens doors, builds muscles and self-confidence, increases flexibility and imagination. It creates new space and time for the work of the spirit; it integrates, enlivens, empowers. It helps us become what we are meant to be, whole persons able to body forth gospel.

Kinesthetic homiletics is not limited to the classroom context. In fact, the group process experience there is intended to be a model of an ongoing pattern of corporate homiletical kinesthesia in the congregational setting. How, then, can participants carry on in this vein in the parish?

Throughout the course, group members are urged to continue doing the warm-up routine on a regular basis, three to five times per week or even daily. It takes only about twenty minutes once fully learned. Over the long term, consistency will likely bear the fruit of a stronger, more flexible, healthier body. Moreover, regular use of the routine helps keep us conscious of movement and provides a ready store of movements and patterns that can be tools in the homiletic enterprise.

The routine can be done to music, but how much better to do it with this week's or next week's sermon text in mind? These and other learned or common movements can be used intentionally to explore words, phrases, and verses—to test out the differences between a ballet walk, a run, a series of lunges or leaps with this word or phrase, or different kinds of turns or rolls with that verse or cluster of verses. Alternately, you can let the Scripture move the body: learn the text, center yourself, attend to what the body wants to do in response to the words, and do it. Put your movements together in sequence and ask yourself what the text is doing, what it is saying, in you. Then identify where those movements connect with people in the congregation and what of the whole can help you in some way to help the community in experiencing this living gospel. At the outset, this work can be integrated with the preacher's preferred pattern of sermon development. Eventually it will come to be the foundation into which other approaches are integrated.

Kinesthetic homiletics can be done in solitude, although that is hardly recommended, but it cannot be done in stillness! To make the group process possible, the pastor can invite an already existing group—a youth group, church council, study group, a series of families—to participate in this experience, or create an entirely new group or series of groups whose sole purpose is homiletical. The limits here are in our imaginations and courage, I submit, more than they are in our congregations. But not having a group with which to work does not preclude moving the text. Nor does inability to move preclude having a group. Indeed, because gospel belongs to everyone, and because gospel is a matter of life or death, we will do everything in our power to work together and aid one another in embodying gospel, embodying God for one another and for the world.

5

Creating a
Full-bodied Sermon

Our kinesthetic homiletic is unapologetically based and centered in Scripture. In the early stages of learning the process we may in fact impose our movements on the pericope. Yet the intention will always be that via the work of the Spirit and the attunement of our bodies/ intellect, the text will move us, interpreting itself through us as whole persons and empowering us to engage in embodied dialogue with it. Furthermore, this homiletic assumes that it is the text that eventually propels us into the library because the passage raises questions that we are not equipped to answer and entices us to attend to all of the factors that brought it to being in the first place. So we apply ourselves to historical/critical methods, not as a way of equipping us to function as plastic surgeons, deconstructing and reconstructing textual anatomy on the basis of outside resources, but as a way of enhancing our ability to receive and comprehend bodily/mentally—wholly—what the text offers us.[1]

We already know that ideas found in the course of traditional exegetical homework may lead to modification of text-based movements. But we are in search of a full-bodied homiletic, and so we will look at the ways in which the data, ideas, and feelings that surface in library research can themselves be explored and experienced through movement. Then, instead of simply carrying the results in our heads and seeking to impress them conceptually upon the textual embodiment, we

---

1. For a useful summary of critical methods, see John H. Hayes and Carl R. Holladay, *Biblical Exegesis: A Beginner's Handbook* (Atlanta: John Knox Press, 1982).

can bring the harvest of our library research *kinesthetically* into conversation with our pericope's choreography.

Moreover, since the preacher, the congregation, the liturgical context, and even the global community are finally integral parts of the homiletic endeavor, we will bodily examine these realities in regard to the particular sermon event. Then, not only the text but everything we bring into dialogue with it will be kinesthetically processed and experienced; our sermon will arise from a wholistic interweaving of all dimensions pertinent to the homiletical enterprise. What follows are some proposals for expanding our kinesthetic homiletic toward this end.[2]

We have seen how quickly our kinesthetic engagement with the text leads us to explore possible movements and meanings of particular words and word groupings. Since we cannot assume, however, that our favorite translation of Scripture offers the best possible presentation of our pericope, it is necessary that we consult other translations and, if possible, the original language of the pericope, giving careful attention to the differences we find. It will not suffice, as we know well by now, to compare and contrast in our heads the Macintosh and Cortland apples, or apples and coconuts, that appear in variants. If we are authentically engaged in our kinesthetic homiletic, the yield of our textual and grammatical criticism will shape itself in our bodies. What does the roundness of all these fruits look like and feel like when we wear it? If we find the Mac mealy and the Cortland crisp, what does that suggest by way of movement? Surely the glossy smoothness of the apple's peel has its home in sustained roundness, while the fuzziness of the coconut may prompt us into almost vibratory scallops!

We will also give the same effort to kinesthetic embodiment of variations in syntax, and be certain to explore physically any words, phrases, or whole verses dropped out of any of our diverse translations. To be sure, even where texts vary in wording or syntax, our movements of these variations may not reveal any particular difference from our original text, because the essence of the text carries through no matter the particular words or grammar supplied by a scribe, editor, or translator. However, the NRSV may indeed evoke a gently nuanced or even significantly different choreography than does its predecessor, for example. When we bring these variant movement patterns into dialogue with previous textual choreography, we may find the pericope's original movement subtly refining or radically reshaping itself as a result of our kinesthetic exploration of variants.

---

2. I do not attempt to discuss every possible hermeneutical aspect and method in what follows. Some things need to be left to the imagination of the reader!

Perhaps the value of this work is more easily seen in the realm of form or literary genre. Particularly when we read aloud, we recognize that we do not read a historical narrative the same way we read most psalms, or an exhortation with the same kind of expression we use for a benediction. Is it not likely, then, that different literary forms will move and impress our kinesthetic sense differently? If we are dealing with dialogue between Peter and Jesus, for example, our embodiment might be framed upon repeated swinging movements that carry us back and forth from one to the other. In contrast, a segment of an epistle that shows the development of an argument might be marked by a studied but nevertheless dramatic change from low intensity to high intensity, or from a very slow, measured pace to a faster-than-we-can-long-maintain tempo. The "begats" may march us along in a tedious, unvarying rhythm, a prophetic oracle may hold us in a suspended lean or lunge while we wait for its fulfillment, or the magnificat while we bask in the warmth and light of post-vision ecstasy.

Yet the purpose of bringing form to embodiment is not to cast each scriptural genre into a set choreographic phrase or quality, but to recognize and live out the truth that the form does inform the text and us kinesthetically, and therefore also our sermon. Having been addressed by and addressing the content of the passage kinesthetically, we will give the same intentional attention to the pericope's form lest our choreography and our sermon limp and wheeze, out of sync and out of balance. Part of what we will learn from this endeavor is what we already know, that form and content cannot be compartmentalized, either in the text or in our homiletical process/event.[3]

We can follow a similar pattern with regard to the pericope's larger literary context. What might be the kinesthetic shape of that which precedes and follows our particular text? How does it inform our text and its embodiment? Does our passage, which previously seemed dull in its motionlessness, now take on a kinesthesia of relieved yet impermanent calm because when we move its literary context we discover the pericope to be the eye of a hurricane? Almost every book of Scripture has a trajectory, a road map for us to follow. Exodus moves us in this direction, Luke-Acts takes us along another route to another place. What would our journey look like and feel like if we embodied it? Is our particular text a rest stop, a dangerous intersection, or all downhill

---

3. Tom Long provides a good summary of the relationship of content and form—which he describes as "the form of the content"—along with some implications of this relationship for preaching. Thomas G. Long, *Preaching and the Literary Forms of the Bible* (Philadelphia: Fortress Press, 1989).

from the mountaintop of transfiguration? Perhaps we might make such a discovery by merely scanning the larger literary unit or imagining it in our mind's eye. But how can we guess cerebrally what the effect on our pericope's kinesthesia will be if the previous material backs into our text and the following content leaps out of it? Moreover, what if this characteristic only surfaces when it moves through us? How much do we miss by applying only our left brain to any part of the homiletical enterprise?

When we come to questions of history, we are reminded that there are two primary dimensions at hand: "internal" and "external" history.[4] The internal history, that which the passage manifests in its content, will in most cases readily be addressed precisely as it meets us in our embodied surrender to the text and its movement of us as we and the pericope explore each other. The external history, which gives occasion to the text, particularly concerns us here. What kind of historical reality would provoke this text, and these movements of us? What might these embodiments tell us about that historical context? As we consult histories and other pertinent sources, we will want to investigate whether those historical particularities bear a particular kind of movement within them. What might it look like to embody the reality of a nation that heard and even saw Jeremiah's prophecies of doom shaped in weaving and pottery (Jer. 13:1-11, 19:1-13) for example? What might it look like to try on the historical context(s) of the seven communities the apocalypticist addresses in Revelation 2–3? What is the kinesthetic difference between the people living under the thumb of the kings who "did evil in the sight of God,"[5] the people living under the thumb of Babylon, the people returned to Israel and living under the thumb of urgent need to rebuild? If we address or are addressed kinesthetically by the historical situation of Romans 15, how might its movement change if we give similar attention to the historical realities of Deuteronomy, the Psalms, and First Isaiah from which Paul quotes? Does our pericope embrace the history in a series of circular patterns? Relevé and tiptoe away from it? Lean toward it and fall into it? Does the history make the text dance? How?

Embodied exegesis is more than a choreography of the words and meanings of a pericope. It includes as well kinesthetic attention to all the dynamics that influenced the building of the text as we know it, as

4. Hayes and Holladay, *Biblical Exegesis*, 42ff.
5. For example, Jehoahaz, 2 Kings 23:31-32; Jehoiakim, 2 Kings 23:36-37; Jehoiachin, 2 Kings 24:8-9.

well as to all the critical methods and their proposals for connecting us with the text. Otherwise half our work healthily integrates mind/body but the remainder resides solely in our heads. The effect is to leave us, the sermon, and the entire homiletical discipline once more disintegrated and incomplete.

But there is more to consider here. Preachers do not come to the homiletical task as if we were so many megabytes of empty memory waiting to be filled up. We come with our own complex history, with our own identity—physical, emotional, intellectual, theological, cultural, and so forth. If you ask me who I am, I might describe myself as five feet five inches tall, a woman of German descent who was raised in the midwestern United States, as a person with a relentlessly inquisitive and ecumenically intrigued mind trained in academic institutions of five different denominational affiliations. I might add that I have a passion for authentic bringing-about of gospel as ongoing, loving dialogical relationship with God and all creation, that I often shake my head in frustration over ecclesial egocentrism and in horror over the absence of justice in the world, that I am disinterested in chess and auto mechanics but love aerobic exercise and baroque music, and that my psychological profile is INFJ (introvert, intuitive, feeling, judging). Similarly, you may describe yourself to me as a thin and bearded male; born, raised in, and narrowly escaped from political imprisonment in China. You may tell me you are infused with a passion for white chocolate and liberation theology, that you grow geraniums but never listen to music or travel if you can avoid it, that you are always smiling and optimistic, that you are awed by the discovery that your efforts to guide your children into healthy, happy, responsible adulthood seem to have borne a splendid outcome (thanks be to God), that your nerves are a bit ajangle about your imminent retirement.

All these kinds of personal dimensions and many, many more we bring to the text and to the sermon each time we are called upon to preach. Yet it is one thing to put who we are into words, and another to attend consciously to our kinesthetic, embodied self-identity. What would it look like if you and I were to allow our bodies to choreograph the essence of our identity—or even if we were to tune our attention to the already existing dance? What surprises might surface, what hidden treasures might be unearthed? Naturally these embodiments are best created in community. My perception, kinesthetic or otherwise, of who I am is only a part of the reality. The rest is shaped by who this community sees/hears/feels me to be.

True, our identities are never static. Who we are today depends not only upon the sum of our existence so far, but also upon whether the sun is shining or rain is falling, upon how much untroubled sleep we got last night and what we ate for breakfast, whether or not our car had a flat on the way to the office, the state of our bank account, and what this text or this community or this world is doing to yesterday's theological/intellectual/emotional/physical perspectives. Yet certainly most of us are far from being chameleons or metamorphs. Much of our self-identity remains stable. Still, we do well to ask from time to time, and perhaps each time we take up a text, "What is going on with me and who am I today?"

We will ask this not only in our heads, but in our bodies. What is the personal choreography we bring to this text, this sermon? Our embodied identity will shape our conversation with the text, like it or not. The fact that we engage in the homiletic enterprise out of three square meals a day, or with a body ravaged by arthritis, or in emotional states that go up and down like a roller coaster; the fact that we participate in this gospel living in Saskatchewan or Texas, at age 57 or 29, makes a real difference. These dynamics provide the refraction and the tint in the lenses through which we see the text, the acoustics in which we hear it; they limit or free us to move this way or that way in response to the pericope. Consequently, it is essential to be consciously, kinesthetically attentive to these realities in order to achieve honest, integrative interface in preaching. Nor should we be surprised if our converse with Scripture redesigns us. After our engagement with any given passage, our personal choreography may take on new dimensions or qualities. Indeed, how could our embodiment *not* be altered by encounter with gospel? Kinesthetic homiletic keeps us in motion, because our lives are in motion, because gospel is.

The same thing is true of our congregations. Faith communities are not all alike, and the disparities may be just as great between one tall-steeple, fat and sassy city congregation and another in the same metropolis as they are between either of those urban groups and the most impoverished deepwoods congregation we can find. At the same time, there may be much in common between many congregations, and perhaps we might one day discover a kind of lowest common denominator choreography that would embody the essence of Christian community. But even if we did, I am not at all convinced it would do us much good.

The fact remains that even though congregations may look alike, they are just not the same.[6]

No doubt we could describe our congregations in all their commonality and uniqueness with reasonable accuracy. But in fact we will not rest with that, any more than we will be satisfied with a mental picture of our personal profile. Our community, our congregation, this collection of the body of Christ, is not made up of mental constructs but of flesh-and-blood bodies that warm the pews and scuff the floors and inhale oxygen and exhale carbon dioxide, thereby causing the candle flames to flicker and the plants to grow. These incarnate lives, individual and corporate, bring theological and cultural, physical and intellectual, emotional and geographical realities to bear on the homiletic enterprise, as we do. These bodies, as we know well, are essential to gospel—and they are essential in their singular uniqueness as well as in their collective uniqueness.

Thus a kinesthetic homiletic will not only include members of the congregation in its processes by inviting them to take an active part in the sermon development, presentation, and assessment—it will also attempt to choreograph the congregation. Better yet, we will invite the congregation, insofar as it is possible, to cast its identity in movement. A preacher's view/embodiment of a community cannot stand apart from the input of its members. That way this mystical, corporate embodiment will intentionally see, sense, and know itself kinesthetically. The preacher and those participating most intensely in this week's sermon development will be able to feel kinesthetically some semblance of who/what this community is—or at least what their perceptions are of what this congregation is like. Otherwise this congregation, even if we keep them in mind throughout the homiletical process, all too easily stays only in mind, lives for us (apart from individual members participating in this sermon's development) in relation to this sermon only in the abstract. Perhaps, then, the congregation will finally live the sermon not at all, because by neglecting their embodiment we have failed to fully discover who they are and therefore do not succeed in connecting this gospel with the *whole* of who these people are. What can happen when we bring the kinesthetic expression of the essence of this congregation into

---

6. For a helpful address of the dimensions shaping each congregation into a unique identity, see James F. Hopewell, *Congregation: Stories and Structure* (Philadelphia: Fortress Press, 1987). Important considerations of the relationship between congregation and the preaching enterprise can be found in Van Seters, *Preaching as a Social Act*, and John S. McClure, *The Four Codes of Preaching: Rhetorical Strategies* (Minneapolis: Fortress Press, 1991).

active interchange with our embodied text-on-the-way-to-being-a-sermon? To our perception of the congregation? To the sermon? To ourselves and the people in the pew?

It will come as no surprise, either, that a similar embodiment needs to be made of the sense(s) we as preacher and people have of the world around us, this incredible ecosystem that is not unaffected by what we say, do, and are. If we think that the world is an environment hostile to the poor, what might we learn by physically exploring that thought? What is the connection between the embodiment of that view and this text, this sermon? If we permit this pericope, this sermon on 1 John to transform our embodiment of the world-as-hostile-environment, what might that offer us by way of vision or impetus for living out this sermon? "Little children, love one another." How can we do this when the world surrounding us is more than happy to eat us alive, to run us down and leave us but a shadow on the pavement, all without even noticing? How might our preaching during the recent months have been transfigured if we had embodied our perceptions of the Serbian people, the Croatian people, the Somali people, the U.S. or Canadian people?

What happens if we not only feel the weight of our own bodily truth,[7] but seek to do the same for truth incarnate in others? At the very least, we may discover how limited we are, how many stereotypes and assumptions we carry around and permit to infect and inhibit or even mutate our relationship with gospel. Such reality is much harder to ignore when it impresses itself upon us kinesthetically than when we can keep it tucked away safely in the corners of our brains. The truth can set us free, it is said. All the more so, kinesthetic homileticians find, when it is felt in their bones and muscles, in their out-of-breath-ness and integratedness of mind/body. Is it not incarnational theology that we are all about?

Sermons are not preached in a vacuum. They most commonly come to reality amidst hymn and prayer; they typically come to life in the context of liturgy. I use this term in the broad sense of all those activities beside the preaching event that may occur on a Sunday morning, including Scripture readings, offering, bath, meal, affirmation of faith, and so on. This liturgy need not be formal in either content or order. It may arise spontaneously, it may be informed by an acknowledged or unacknowledged tradition, or it may be sculpted and set long in advance either by this community or by a denominational committee on the other side of the continent or world. In any case, whatever else we intend to

---

7. Troeger, *Imagining*, 53f.

carry out as a gathered community around the preaching event both informs and is informed by the homiletical enterprise.[8]

Thus, our homiletical enterprise needs to be conscious of the impact of its liturgical context from start to finish. That means that we attend to the character of that liturgical setting not just in our heads but in our muscles, bones, nerve endings. How would we move to communicate to a deaf person what this "liturgy" that will be the context of this sermon is all about? What is the kinesthesia of this gathering when we will meet for prayer and song, word/act, conversation/choreography that constitutes us Christians?

Here we may have much help by virtue of the fact that we already in some way move baptism and supper; we stand up, sit down, perhaps kneel or process up or down the aisle, or reach out to greet one another with the handclasp or hug of peace. Movement and worship events are no strangers. On the other hand, these patterned actions may be a hindrance because their actuality carries with it all sorts of presuppositions. What if we were to choreograph the giving of bread and the fruit of the vine anew? More correctly, what might we discover about this meal if we permitted it to move us? What if we would let the peace actually make us, well, peaceful? What might happen if we were to allow the baptismal event to shape itself all over again on our bodies?

I am not talking about rebaptism here, or even affirmation of baptism, but rather a rediscovery of the physicality of these events, of their kinesthetic sense, of the effect of these embodiments on our pericope/ sermon, and on us. What does the way in which we do things on a Sunday morning—greet one another, confess our sin, receive again the declaration of pardon, read and hear Scripture, affirm our faith—look and feel like when we grant these acts their rightful potency to act on us and move us? What effects do those patterns of motion have in conjunction with our text-based movement? Similarly, if the season is

---

8. I do not agree with Charles Rice about the relationship between sermon and liturgy. A kinesthetic homiletic embodies gospel in the sermon in a way that is closely akin to the embodiment of gospel in bath and meal. Both of these, along with other liturgical acts and preaching, are intimate parts of the whole worship event. All the elements of such an event can and do embody gospel, and no simplistic division between God's part and ours can be made. Moreover, if gospel is embodied in preaching, can we continue to retain the classic distinction between "word" and "sacrament"? Finally, neither sermon nor meal is the end of anything, but the beginning of lives lived out in the world, embodiments of gospel-God in the world. Perhaps true sacrament is embodied gospel-God lived out in pulpit and pet store, at table and in the laboratory. Nevertheless, Rice offers some valuable thoughts on strengthening the relationship between homiletics and liturgy. Charles L. Rice, *The Embodied Word: Preaching as Art and Liturgy* (Minneapolis: Fortress Press, 1991).

Advent, what shape does that take kinesthetically? What is the difference if it is the fourth Sunday of Lent? Trinity Sunday? Or "just another green Sunday"? How do those choreographies and embodiments dance with the dance of our text?[9]

Our kinesthetic homiletic can also feed and nurture our liturgy. Particular embodiments or movement patterns choreographed by the text yet not finally belonging to the sermon can create fresh prayers or hymn texts, or point us to existing ones that we might not otherwise have remembered or considered using. Similarly, the movement of our text may define the movement of the liturgy; perhaps on occasion the sequence of liturgical steps will flow directly from sermon to supper or baptism without pausing for hymn or affirmation of faith or taking up the collection or any of the other many elements that may normally occur between. Perhaps the sermon will be so informed by the liturgical choreography, and the liturgy will be so impacted by our kinesthetic homiletic, that the sermon will swirl around the baptism, or the prayers of the people or the sharing of peace will find its home in such immediate vicinity of the sermon that the idea of good fencing making good neighbors will simply not apply.[10]

Or perhaps no such dramatic transformations of the worship event may occur. Instead we may find only a quiet growth of integrity between sermon and liturgy that increasingly strengthens congregations in gospel experience and empowers them as individual members and as a whole body to live out gospel more and more in all they do and everywhere they go. If that growth is to take place, however, we will need to give all the aspects of the worship event—sermon, supper, creed, announcements(!)—their kinesthetic due and freedom to be informed by and to inform the kinesthesia of each other.

What we seek here is to draw the people in the pew increasingly into full-bodied participation in gospel event as manifested in the start-to-finish work of kinesthetic homiletic become kinesthetic liturgy. A kinesthetic homiletic, and a kinesthetic liturgy that arises from it and from

9. Like texts themselves, personal, congregational, global, and liturgical identities are complex. Each no doubt deserves a suite of dances. In the same way we finally express the essence of a text into its nutshell state prior to shaping it into a sermon, we will likewise need to streamline our embodiments of identity into concentrated form.

10. Robert Frost, "Mending Wall." I agree with the poet, not the neighbor, and prefer the beginning lines, "Something there is that doesn't love a wall, That sends the frozen ground swell under it, And spills the upper boulders in the sun; And makes gaps even two can pass abreast." And again, "Before I built a wall I'd ask to know What I was walling in or walling out, And to whom I was like to give offense. Something there is that doesn't love a wall, That wants it down." Yes. Oscar Williams and Edwin Honig, eds., *The Mentor Book of Major American Poets* (New York and Scarborough, Ontario: New American Library, 1962), 235–36.

its own embodiment of gospel, are not about forcing our community to perform our steps and rhythms, predesigned or improvised on the spot. Imposing even small change, let alone dramatic change, "from on high" does violence both to the community and to gospel, which mediates against hierarchy and tyranny and calls and empowers us to shape our life together from the inside out. Thus this kinesthetic enterprise, like gospel, aims at empowering our people to experience and embrace the freedom that gospel provides us to be who we are meant to be—fully embodied, integrated, whole participants in the loving, graceful choreography of God.

Our kinesthetic homiletic and its sibling liturgy do present significant challenges, challenges that have to do with more than our out-of-practice muscles and ligaments and our two left feet. This enterprise takes to court the notions that there is one right way to do liturgy; that liturgy and preaching have one correct relationship; that preaching is God's word to us and liturgy our response; that preaching is the sole responsibility of the designated preacher and liturgical design the exclusive responsibility of knowledgeable professionals; that Sunday mornings (or whenever Christians gather for worship) and our Christian life of faith itself have to do primarily with our heads. When gospel enlivens us wholly, when gospel claims us in our DNA and in our ligaments, in our olfactory sense and in our nerve endings and not just in our ears, a lot of the rules defined by various traditions and habits, theological or otherwise, begin to change or even to evaporate. Gospel designs our individual lives and our lives together around new patterns, processes, and movements. This is so because gospel itself is not static but dynamic, and therefore our relationship with God, each other, and the whole creation is always, if only subtly, on the move. If we are faithful to it, gospel will not permit us long to rest on our status quos, for we are ever beckoned/whirled by the Spirit into new ways of being, doing, relating, even as we are confronted by our global ecosystem to adjust to the new realities it daily sets before us.

Yet some things, we trust, will never change. The love of God for us and God's loving presence with us, and our absolute dependence on both of those realities, will remain the ground and center of our whole being. What changes is how we embody that reality for ourselves and so for others—on a Sunday morning, in the library or at the supermarket, amidst terrible famines in Africa, in the face of plagues like AIDS, as a counter to domestic and global violence and warfare. Our kinesthetic homiletic is not a miracle cure for our past or present failures in authentically living gospel. But it can move us toward wholeness, because it honors the whole reality God so deeply loves and empowers us to embody God for the world—to be the hands, face, kinesthesia of God that stand between the world and death in order to create life.